Easy Counselling Essays

By Francis Reuben Sturt. BSc Hons, Dip. Couns & Psych.

._____

"Great Read...excellent book and easy to understand...value for money..."
Ruby D. Amazon Reviewer. *Based on a review of Volume 1.*

"Do you like things to be simple? If you do, you will love this book."

It is a compelling selection of "back to basics", easy to read, argumentative essays, that are mostly free of "scary" jargon.

Is it for you? Yes, if you have a little knowledge of counselling theory or practice and it is ideal for those of you at, a mature age, studying GCSE or "A" levels.

What makes a good counsellor? Take this excerpt from Assignment 1, " ...a valuable and effective counsellor is, one of high ethical standards, a good listener, has empathy, and holds the client in absolute positive regard..."

Written from a Humanistic/Integrative, theoretical perspective,it has you the reader in mind throughout the essays. A simple, uncomplicated, refreshing introduction to the fundamentals of counselling that should provide the knowledge and skills necessary for further study.

It is also an informative guide to counselling for those of you, who simply wish to have a greater understanding of oneself or others.

The 10 assignments include:eating disorders; anxiety; depression; phobias; self harm; sexuality; case studies;session plans and lots more!

It was worth all the effort to give you an easy to read collection of argumentative essays that were rewarded with a "Distinction."

I hope sincerely that they help with your studies and if you are reading for pleasure; have an enjoyable and satisfying read.

Francis R Sturt. BSc Hons. Dip.Couns & Psych.

ISBN-13: 9781539457190
ISBN-10: 1539457192

My Assignments

============

1. p4 The differences between counselling and psychotherapy, being an effective counsellor and the necessary conditions needed to see a counsellor.

Assignment 1

_____

Q1.1

I will study,define and contrast in detail the two therapies: psychotherapy and counselling.The Royal College of Psychiatry defines psychotherapy as a talking treatment, between a psychotherapist and a client.

Counselling is a regular treatment on a weekly or more basis, usually lasting up to 50 minutes per session. Psychotherapy may last for a month, up to a year or more, depending on the severity of the client's distress or on how deep rooted the condition may be. For example, a neurosis, such as anxiety concerning parenting difficulties will probably require less sessions, than a psychosis, such as paranoia. A psychosis is usually deep rooted and may begin in early childhood.

Generally the more traumatic the client's experience is, such as sexual abuse, the more in depth and longer the treatment will last.

Psychotherapy is a "healing relationship" held in privacy and is always highly confidential, except when a criminal or suicidal act is made. Then a referral is made to an outside agency or professional, such as the police or an NHS Psychiatrist,,as in the case of suspected child abuse.

Psychotherapy is an in-depth and psychodynamic, "healing of the soul." The therapist needs to understand the dynamic relationships between childhood trauma and the client's presenting disorders, e.g. the abused client may show symptoms of trauma, PTSD, or depression.

Counselling is similar to psychotherapy in that it is a "talk and listen" therapy, but counselling is mostly listening and problem solving,e.g. finding employment and stress related redundancies.

Counselling is also confidential between client and counsellor, although the therapist may consult a supervisor, who deals with client issues: anger and violence. The supervisor may also listen to problems the client has with the therapist. e.g. racial prejudice and transference.

The counsellor may ask the client to contact other professionals or agencies, such as a careers advisor for job training or a psychiatrist for antidepressants and tranquilizers.,e.g. Diazepam, Prozac etc.

The counsellor will help the client find practical solutions to their dissatisfaction and loss of direction, such as financial difficulties and feelings of helplessness in finding employment.

Counsellors are mostly concerned with present difficulties and related neurosis, e.g. fear of failure or anxiety due to stress.

Both therapies require good, client-therapist trustful, relationships, as well as an ability to explore and discuss thoughts, feelings and behaviour in a safe and confidential setting.
They differ only in the depth of analysis, e.g. serious sexual abuse may require an analysis of early childhood traumas. Such abuse may lead to severe mental illness, such as Borderline Personality Disorder(BPD). schizophrenia and lack of contact with reality: delusions, hallucinations etc.

Psychosis is seen by Psychotherapists and Psychiatrists and not counsellors in general. However, some counsellors do specialise with a psychosis, such as schizophrenia. Medication may be required.

Sexual identity difficulties and Posttraumatic Stress Disorders(PTSD) require in-depth psychotherapy. Listening counselling here may have little benefit to the client. Again, some counsellors may help with clients coping with PTSD.

Psychotherapy is good for treating psychosis and deep-rooted, childhood experiences and trauma; where in-depth analysis is necessary and longer periods of analysis are vital for mental health.

Q1.2

I will study the value of the basic key requirements to be an effective counsellor.

Essentially a counsellor needs to be stable, secure and mentally confident to be able to give her undivided attention to the client. Failure to meet these criteria indicates that the counsellor is not ready to practice her counselling skills.

The counsellor needs thorough practical "face to face" training, which may be on a one -to - one or group basis. This need not to be simply in a face - to - face, personal therapy room, telephone and webcam dialogues may be acceptable too.

The training should lead to a recognised qualification, such as an OCN diploma, a graduates degree or a Masters post graduate degree. All training should relate the theoretical to the specific practical setting.

Practical training should ideally be accredited by a governing body or counselling organisation, such as the BACP or the Counselling Society.

A professional body such as the British Association of Counsellors and Psychotherapists should provide professional, moral and ethical codes of practice,e.g. a separation between the private and public domains of counsellor and client, such as a strict code of the counsellors' restricted availability, outside the agreed therapy "hour".

This code should be studied by the client and both parties should accept the therapy governing conditions, before any counselling takes place.

The counsellor should have a thorough grasp of the different counselling tools and skills, including a working knowledge of the various therapeutic approaches,e.g. CBT, DBT, Gestalt etc

The counsellor's skills should include an ability to have empathy, emotional warmth, in-depth knowledge, and possess good listening skills and emotional stability and confidence.

Counselling and psychotherapy are both "talk and listen" methods requiring non-judgemental, inclusive, impartial, non-partisan skills and strategies.

Confidentiality and honesty is paramount in therapy and without it trust and faith in the counsellor could evaporate, leading possibly to the client ending the therapy. The proper ending of the client's therapy should be clear and agreed upon from the start of therapy and adequate notice of termination by the counsellor should be given.

Self awareness or "mindfulness" of one's own limitations and projections, may prevent transferences that have no truth in reality, e.g. the counsellor one's own feelings and experiences of men as always "unreliable", on to the client. Awareness of invaluable learnt and intuitive abilities may prevent bias and prejudices in therapy sessions. Thus maintaining the therapist's impartiality.

To summarise a valuable and effective counsellor is, one of high ethical standards, a good listener, has empathy, holds the client in absolute positive regard and is highly trained and has a range of therapeutic skills and tools.

Assignment 1.3

I intend to study and detail the conditions for which it would be appropriate for a client to see a counsellor or a psychotherapist.

Firstly, the client must be suffering from a mental disorder, such as a neurosis or psychosis, or have a specific mental problem, crisis or difficulty requiring solutions.

The client seeking therapy should come by their own free will, exceptions to this rule may include "sectioning" under the Mental Health Act, where therapy is a compulsory part of treatment. Young people under 16 may need support from their family and be accompanied by an adult parent or guardian.

The mental disorders, requiring in-depth understanding of the psycho-dynamics underlying mental illness, may range from depression to personality disorders, to specific problems requiring less intensive guided counselling: redundancy, eviction, exam stress, etc.

A client suffering from a severe mental disorder, such as a personality disorder, should first see their GP or psychiatrist, who may refer the client to a counsellor or psychotherapist.

Indeed, the client may have received medication by a psychiatrist; such as antidepressants for major depressive illness, and not been cured. The psychiatrist may deal with the symptoms and not the causes of depression, which may lie with early childhood traumas.
So, a psychiatric treatment may have been said to have failed by the client and is a good enough reason to seek counselling.

The client may seek therapy to create a strong Adult ego state, to allow for alternative conceptions and reasoning, such as re-evaluating an experience of abuse as the fault of the abuser, rather than that of a "guilty" abused client. The client may present herself with self-accusation and guilt when first undergoing counselling.

Again, the client would almost certainly need the aid of a therapist to support her own resources, e.g. re-evaluation of trauma(s), to help the patient see that she is innocent and the abuser is "guilty."

A condition for successful counselling is guidance by the therapist, based on the client's own resources. It has to be said that a client seeking greater awareness of her own psyche and mental abilities, is in itself a good reason for entering therapy. This is particularly true of patients who have tried traditional psychiatric or other complementary therapies for depression, anxiety etc, and had negative outcomes.

Therefore, there are many appropriate conditions for someone to seek counselling or psychotherapy. But, above all else, the client needs to understand counselling is about listening and talking on a therapeutic basis and applying relevant new coping strategies, agreed with her therapist. Indeed, the client's need to understand personal growth and a happy Adult-Child ego relationship in her mind, are valid reasons and appropriate conditions to see a therapist or counsellor.

================================

Assignment 2

_____

Q2.1/

Cognitive Behaviour Therapy was developed in the 1960's by Aaron Beck, as an integrated talking therapy for major mental disorders, such as depression; anxiety, delusions; eating disorders etc.

CBT is based on the theory that cognition, emotions and behaviour are all interrelated. This is demonstrated by a cycle of negative thinking- negative moods- negative behaviour leading to more negative thinking.

CBT aims to help clients interrupt and eventually break this negative cycle by a therapist challenging and questioning the logic behind such statements as, "I will never find a girlfriend". Therapist asks, "Is this reasonable? "Yes, because women always reject me". Therapist asks, "Is there a good reason for letting go of this thought?" and client may reply, "Yes, because I would be more positive and confident when approaching women". Therapist may ask, "What is the worst outcome?" and the client may reply, "I fail to date a woman". Therapist asks, "How would you cope?" Client replies, "Perhaps by going to an assertiveness class or simply keep chatting to women and practicing my social skills".

CBT then challenges misinterpretations of situations and others' actions or speech. The client re-evaluates his misinterpretations and replaces his negative cycle of thought, emotions and behaviour, with a more realistic and positive cognitive outlook. This breaks his anxiety and restores his well being.

CBT usually takes place on a weekly, one-to-one basis, or as in a group and is generally considered a short term treatment lasting a few months to a year, depending on the client's situation, commitments and the severity of her mental disorder.

N.I.C.E. stands for the National Institute for Health and Clinical Excellence. NICE is defined as an, "Independent body offering clinical guidelines for treatment or therapy for diseases or disorders". This includes mental disorders, such as depression and anxiety.

The main reason why N.I.C.E. recommends CBT for treatment of minor or major mental disorders is because of the benefits to clients listed below.

CBT is considered cost-effective, when compared to funding long-term medication. CBT is brief, usually a few months to a year. CBT deals with the psycho-dynamics of anxiety, depression, PTSD, etc. It is a more effective treatment, than psychiatric drugs, as it seeks to find a solution to the negative cycle of thinking, emotions and behaviour. Most medication doesn't cure the disorder, but only deals with suppressing symptoms. e.g. phobias concerning dogs perceived as being "dangerous".

Like phobias, CBT is effective for most major mental disorders, except perhaps schizophrenia. A schizophrenic may lack the mental stability or strong adult ego to understand the cognitive therapy. However, as with most mental disorders, the adult ego may be weak at the beginning of treatment and unlike drugs; it can be strengthened by CBT.

Clinical trials have proven that the patient's mental health is sustained, even after 2 years since CBT and there are fewer relapses when compared to medication. There is little restimulation in the CBT process due to the fact that CBT focuses mainly on the present. So NICE approves of its effects.

Q2.2/

Solution Focused Therapy or SFBT is a talking treatment between a therapist and a client. SFT is based on a constructionist philosophy and is therefore well structured. It focuses on the client's goals, rather than the problems that brought them to therapy in the first place.

SFT as an isolated therapy aims to elicit the client's own skills and resources, largely by a series of questions. The questions are concerned with the present and the future; a comparison between "what is" and "what could be". The past experiences are largely irrelevant. The therapist maintains "respectful curiosity". i.e. the client's story is validated and her resources felicitated by gentle questioning. SFT is based on three major methods: "Preferred Future", "The Miracle Question" and "Problem Free Talk".

The "preferred future" enables the patient to move forward by envisioning a future when illness or presenting problems are absent. The difference between the present and imagined future is what is worked on in therapy.

A series of questions are asked by the therapist to elicit the client's strengths and to help them to reach their own goals. The benefits are small or large scale changes in the client's mental health. Also, the client reinforces good mental health by focusing on "successful" times when distress was not present, and repeating the focus, on those more positive times.

The "Miracle Question" asks how a dream may come true. If the imagined dream; as it applies to the client, envisaged a time, for example, when depression or paranoia is absent - this may give the client goals to move towards.

The client may envisage a time where are they are calm, trusting, and relaxed with healthy psychological functioning. i.e. a valuable insight into a life free from depression or anxiety. The client then classifies their present and dream-like future on a scale from 0 to 10. This scaling is essential if the client is to understand and value, "where they are now", and the value of "where they will be in the future." e.g. 9-10 on the scale. The main value of this is to move the client forward to good mental health and to value positive thoughts and emotions, when in a distressed period. The imagined dream is valuable in freeing up skills and resources that are available to the patient in the present.

"Problem Free Talk", draws on the patient's external resources, such as social activities, relaxation and social networking. In other words to seek from the client times when they were assertive, positive and calm. Thus validating the client's resources in times of distress. e.g. depression.

By using these resources the client moves forward psychologically and resolves conflict and disorders.

Dan Jones described the above process as, "…accessing resources enabling client with goals…" A good example of the Problem Free Talk is one where a parent has a deviant child that does not respond to her demands. The therapist elicits times when the client is obeyed. The patient responds by mentioning that when she takes the dog for a walk, the dog doesn't bark at cats because the client speaks firmly to her dog. The client through prompting realises she is not firm and consistent with her ill behaved child. The therapist asks the client, if the patient used a firmer tone, as she did with the dog, and laid down clear boundaries of acceptable behaviour, the child might improve his behaviour. The value of this is the conflict of discipline, between client and son, may be resolved and the patient would feel less anxious, angry or depressed. Thus a time of no conflict, the dog, is valid for applying to a time when conflict, between client and child, is present.

Solution Focused Therapy is valuable as an isolated treatment because it utilises the client's own resources, internal or external. SFT uses the patient's imagination to realise positive goals, increases confidence and skills in handling difficult situations, resolving conflicts, but a "crisis" may require drugs. SFT is limited by being brief and needs a strong adult ego.

Q2.3/

Dialectical Behaviour Therapy was developed in the 1960's by Marsha Linehan, primarily for those who self harm and are diagnosed as having Border Personality Disorder. It is dialectical in the sense that it counter balances the negative symptoms of BPD, by mainly utilising CBT and Zen Mindfulness on a one-to-one basis with a DBT trained therapist or in groups, also by telephone links. The sessions take place over a year or more, usually for an hour on a weekly basis. In the sessions the client is encouraged to take control of their emotions, by a series of therapeutic stages and a hierarchy of targets. Therefore the therapy is well structured and each stage or target is well defined. Both strategies, CBT and mindfulness are aimed at challenging negative behaviour, such as self harm and suicidal tendencies. Therefore, building behavioural skills to reduce the symptoms stated. DBT is therefore defined as an effective treatment for BPD sufferers and for those who self harm or commit antisocial acts. e.g. law breaking.

Border Personality Disorder was developed as a major disability over the last 50 years and as the term suggests it is a serious disorder of both neurotic and psychotic symptoms. But is better defined as an inability to control emotions and conform to the appropriate behaviour of the majority in any society. Of course these rules may vary from one culture to another. e.g. anger may be expressed more easily in Middle East, moslem, countries, but has to be suppressed in social situations in Western Europe, such as in bereavement where "wailing" and "shouting" is less common.

BPD is characterised by "…significant instability of Interpersonal relationships, self image, mood and impulsive behaviour."

There is a substantial impairment of social, occupational and psychological functioning. These dysfunctions are best described by P.R.A.I.S.E., where there is significant paranoia, relationship malfunctioning, outward displays of anger or violence to people or property, impulsive behaviour which may lead to breaking laws, self-harm or suicidal tendencies and feelings of emptiness. BPD has many aspects of other mental disorders, such as schizophrenia, where paranoia, is more prevalent.. If BPD is to be taken seriously, then the P.R.A.I.S.E symptoms should apply together and not dependent on a sole symptom e.g. paranoia..

The benefits of DBT for BPD sufferers are many and varied. DBT is valid because it is specifically designed for BPD clients and therefore it cuts out any irrelevant techniques, such as NLP. Where extensive Socratic questioning is involved, this may promote paranoia, if the client feels "interrogated.". The BPD client learns to become "mindful" of their behaviour and how it affects other people or property. Fear of abandonment leading to breakdown of trust in relationship and the fear manifesting itself as an outcome,e.g. a fear of abandonment based on a client's mother withdrawing love and protection, as a child, leading to mistrust of the opposite sex in adult relationships and relationship breakdowns - separation and divorce. Mindfulness relies less on thought and more on reflective awareness of the outside world, so there is little pondering on negative thoughts creating a negative mood or behaviour.

Through the dialectical process the client identifies problem behaviour, such as self-harm, and is countered by understanding. DBT has a proven record of less self harm and less time spent in Psychiatric units. This is mainly due to increased awareness and emotional control skills. Indeed, the BPD client is expected to take responsibility for what they can do and should not do in social or private situations. The client therefore retakes control of her life and resolves the problem thoughts, emotions and behaviour. This is the value of the dialectical response.

The other benefits of DBT to BPD clients are recorded success in keeping patients in therapy and less suicidal recurrences, mainly because the client is validated and met with compassion. Also, the client is usually able to receive care between sessions. E.g. training, education and helpline contacts.

If the help is by telephone then the client may remain anonymous and feel less inhibited, when talking freely about their issues. The telephone client may choose a time that is suitable for them and at a location far from drop-in centres or psychiatric units, where the client may feel inhibited by perceived eavesdropping.

Although the patient may feel less vulnerable, calling from her bedroom or in private on a mobile phone, there are limitations: the therapist is unable to read body language and is dependent wholly on what the client says, tone of voice, silences etc

Suicidal intent may not be always be easily identified without a good understanding of the clients moods; an experienced therapist is far more likely to perceive any threat by understanding the client's unresolved conflicts. E.g. unexpressed grief or anger following the death of a close friend or relation.

In the hierarchy of targets and stages; suicidal intent or attempts come first in therapy. If suicide or self harm presents itself, then it must be dealt with before applying any other skill or target. Any threat or talk of suicide should be taken seriously. Each target or skill must be reached before moving on to the next stage; from decreasing suicidal intent to dealing with Post Traumatic Stress Disorder. Thereby actual suicide is prevented, as the causes are challenged before it is too late!

PTSD may be encountered by identifying possible sexual, physical or emotional abuse and realising the connections with present behaviour. E.g. relationship difficulties with partners. Dialectical resolution takes place and the client gains a better quality of life. The limitations of DBT when treating BPD clients are mainly one of excluding patients with eating or alcohol or substance abuse. This is poor because eating and drug misuse are a symptom of personality disorder. In addition, the targets and skill stages depend on a strong adult ego state for it to be effective and understood.

With many BPD sufferers they lack emotional maturity and have a powerful child ego. I.e. they think and act like small children. In talking treatments there is a strong tendency to think the way out of problems or difficulties, this may result in excessive negative thought leading to bad moods and more negative thoughts.

The limitation here is one of neglecting the theory that mood always comes first and thoughts follow. Many therapists may actually cause the client to spend years in therapy because of asking the patient to think through the past childhood; too traumatic for some whom have experienced severe sexual or physical abuse.

Therefore, all that may arguably be achieved is more negative thinking and the moods remaining intact. In other words, the client may progress more quickly if they are shown that thoughts have no life of their own, except what significance the person gives it. The thoughts are "real", but do not represent "reality".

To conclude DBT has a testable theory of effectiveness where BPD sufferers are concerned. It may be effective and benefit most BPD clients, but its greatest flaw is that it excludes patients with eating disorders, solvent abuse etc. The scope of definition of BPD may be too wide, as it has features that overlap with major illnesses. E.g. paranoia belonging to schizophrenia and feelings of emptiness and self harm belonging to major depression. The strength of DBT may lie with its eclecticism and highly structured techniques. I.e. skills and targets. These techniques are highly beneficial in altering behavioural and emotional patterns of distress. E.g. suicidal feelings.

Mindfulness may benefit the patient more because it would focus on the negative effects of suicide on the client's loved ones or friends. Overall the BPD client benefits from a therapy that is practical, achievable and has healthy psychological functioning as its aim.

=================================

ASSIGNMENT 3

_____

1. Evaluate the benefits and any other impact of at least 5 psychiatric drugs and the conditions for which they might be most usefully prescribed.

I intend to answer this question by using a fictitious client, named Fred, as a case study for a worsening mental disorder and his treatment by 5 psychiatric drugs.

PARSTELIN

#MANERIX

#LARGACTIL

#OLANZAPINE

#DIAZEPAM

a/ PARSTELIN

============

Fred is made redundant from his plasterers job with his local council and begins to suffer reactive depression and some anxiety.

Fred sees a GP and is prescribed Parstelin.

The benefits for Fred are reduced anxiety and less severe depressions.

The drug enables Fred to carry out a new job due to the antidepressant and stimulant effect of the medication. However, in other cases the drug has a sedative effect and may numb feelings about the client's own reality. Usually Parstelin is prescribed when over Tricyclic drugs fail, but Fred's GP feels that the combination of a sedative and antidepressant is ideal for Fred's anxiety about being a perfectionist at work and his depression about "not being good enough." Many Psychiatrists, however, feel that that MAOI combination drugs are too crude, inaccurate and don't respect the individual's needs of the patient. There are other benefits too, such as Parstelin has anticonvulsant properties and has a controlling effect on emotions and pain.

Fred unfortunately consumes a great amount of cheese and Chianti wine. As a result he begins to suffer from high blood pressure and his doctor strongly recommends he gives up his cheese and wine due to interactions with Tyramine; a natural chemical found in the body.

After some time on Parstelin, Fred suffers side effects, such as increased nervousness, reduced sexual feelings, dry mouth, headaches, and blurred vision. These side effects are common and may manifest themselves early in treatment, as Parstelin is quick acting. (MIND)
The other uses of MAOIs are: can be combined with other sedatives, such as Stelazine, and antidepressants.e.g. Prothiaden. Parstelin sedative effect may be useful for BPD sufferers, especially in regards to anger and self harm.

It seems that Parstelin is considered as unsafe because of its harmful interactions with Tyramine and the need to restrict one's diet. Fred finds these restrictions too excessive, so his GP refers Fred to a Psychiatrist.

3b/ MANERIX

Fred's Psychiatrist signs Fred off from full-time work, but as Manerix is prescribed to stabilise Fred's moods and deepening depression, he is made redundant from another job as a painter. Fred is beginning to suffer some persecution feelings, as Fred believes he has been made unemployed without good reason, due to a perceived plot to dismiss him, by his colleagues at work.. Fred is more anxious about his future and also feels that he is a failure at work. Although Fred is conscientious and hardworking in employment.

Manerix affects the levels of serotonin and dopamine, the happy hormones, in the brain, therefore relieving Fred from black depressions. Wikipedia states that MAOIs, "block the decomposition of serotonin and dopamine" in the mind, thus boosting mood and good health.

Fred is able to reintroduce cheese and small amounts of alcohol in his diet, as Manerix does not react to Tyramine, except arguably in excessive amounts of Tyramine rich food. Although Manerix is considered a safer, modified MAOI, compared to its predecessors Parstelin and Parnate, it is unsuitable for most elderly people as it may cause strokes, walking difficulties and even death. (Lilly 2008). However, these extreme cases are very rare and empirical evidence of their frequency is lacking. It is also largely unsuitable for pregnant women.

Babies may be born with "tremors, over tired and drowsy." Lilly 2008 Although other factors of causation must be taken into account e..g. Hereditary and genetic influences.

Manerix may also cause aggressiveness, agitation and dizziness. (APS 2001) It has to be said that these extreme symptoms are rare and Fred is happy with his new medication as a powerful anti-depressant. Fred's persecutory complex is now manifesting itself as social phobia and Manerix enables Fred to socialise, work voluntary, and enjoy his favourite activity: gardening. Fred also forms a self-help group for fellow sufferers with social anxiety; a fear of people and places. He is able to reduce his phobia by sharing his experiences and by getting support and encouragement from the group, that helps him face up to his fears.

Manerix like other MAOIs is seen as a last resort to treat major depression and anxiety, especially social phobias, by most Psychiatrists. It is fast working as "it is rapidly digested in the gut." It is less sedating than typical antidepressants and is enabling. However, some minor diet restrictions and a possible reduction of platelets in one's blood, is a cause for some concern. Fred now works, a few voluntary hours, in a charity shop. But, unfortunately Fred's wife is unfaithful and this leads to a divorce. Fred who loved his wife has a major nervous breakdown, after disposing of his medication, and is hospitalised in a local psychiatric unit.

3/c LARGACTIL

Fred reveals his fear that he is being followed by the Russian KGB and the TV personality Ben Elton, whom he feels respectively, are either going to kill him or interview him on TV. Fred now has major delusions and hallucinations.

Fred is hearing the voice of Ben Elton and seeing men in black suits, everywhere he goes. On one occasion Fred visits his local police station in a terrified state and claims that a man in a black is threatening him with a knife in the High Street. The police report the incident to the psychiatric unit and he is sectioned under the Mental Health Act. At this time Fred is refusing all medication. The very medication that may have presented his breakdown and psychotic state.

Fred's psychiatrist diagnoses him as schizophrenic and, then prescribes anti-psychotics.. The benefits to Fred are that his hallucinations and delusions are suppressed. He also is sedated by Chlorpromazine (Largactil), which helps Fred to sleep and remain calm. However, the Largactil renders Fred almost impotent, gives him terrific weight gain, affects his esophagus, and that causes him gastric-reflux. Chlorpromazine arguably causes more latent ill effects, that may be more difficult to handle than his psychotic illness itself alone. The therapist would need to take into account the pros and cons of the presenting illness and the medication's side effects, before seriously considering counselling a client, like Fred, and may need advice from the client's psychiatrist.

.Fred, immediately, after his divorce felt suicidal and self-harmed himself by scolding himself with boiling water. Largactil reduces his suicidal and self-harm tendencies, principally by sedating him, so Fred can't find the energy to attempt destructive behaviour The price of this sedated, drowsy, sleepiness state, maybe months, if not years of somewhat comatose idleness and that may render counselling useless, as Fred's cognitive functioning may be severely impaired by psychosis and drugs..

The other impacts on Fred are he is so sedated, that he cannot function socially, vocationally or relate to his family. In fact he is now mostly prostrate in his hospital bed. Fred cannot work and feels little energy to do therapeutic tasks. I.e. occupational therapy. Indeed, Mind states that Largactil is "…more sedating…than any other antipsychotic…"

Fred's symptoms do not totally disappear and he feels strongly that there are listening devices in his ward. This is typical of psychotic delusions, however any powerfully held beliefs are better met with absolute positive regard and not dismissed willy-nilly. The frustration of not being taken seriously has the effect of inducing despair and depression, leaving the client all alone in a nightmarish world, one he feels unable to escape from.The Psychiatrist increases the dose of Chlorpromazine to 1000 mg, a controversial dose that can cause death in some elderly patients. It relieves the paranoia that Fred feels but his weight gain is considerable; from 15 to 19 Kgs and his appetite is over-stimulated, adding even greater weight gain.. Patients, like Fred, feel little benefit in exercising regularly, as it seemingly makes little difference to their obesity and well being.

Fred begins to vomit frequently, possibly due to the controversial dose of 1gm of chlorpromazine.

However, the doctor suggests Fred's heavy smoking of over 40 cigarettes per day is the main cause of his reflux and consequently prescribed nicotine patches. The Psychiatrist sends Fred for tests and this establishes that Fred has oesophageal damage, causing vomiting.

It is debatable, as to whether the drugs caused the oesophagus complications. But, it has been established that, "…overeating, weight gain, a slowing down of mental alertness, sunburn…" are major side effects of Largactil. Tardive Dyskinesia and liver failure are also longer term side effects. (MIND). However, it is interesting to note that Chlorpromazine is occasionally used as a treatment for nausea.It remains that 1gm doses of Chlorpromazine are highly disputed among medical professionals.

Clearly in Fred's case Largactil does relieve delusions and represses hallucinations, therefore it is a powerful antipsychotic for schizophrenia and other major mental disorders. I.e. schizoaffective disorder and bipolar disorder. It is also a powerful agent in the treatment of antisocial behaviour, such as self harm and law breaking. So, as a sedative it may help sufferers of BPD, with a history of aggression and/or impulsive antisocial violence towards themselves or property.

3/d OLANZAPINE

After 16 weeks in a psychiatric unit, Fred is discharged on the condition he attends a Psychiatric Day Hospital on a twice- weekly basis.

Fred is now drinking alcohol heavily and smoking again. He visits his new Psychiatrist and complains of being too heavily sedated, drowsy and lacking in energy. Fred is keen to resume some form of work.

Luckily for Fred he is told by his doctor that a new antipsychotic has been made available by NICE and that it has less side-effects than Chlorpromazine: namely Zyprexa or Olanzapine. Fred is prescribed the highest level of the new drug: 20 mg a day.

The benefits are that Fred's fear of being persecuted is suppressed and his hallucinations and deluded thoughts are dissipated. Fred no longer believes that Ben Elton is out to expose his private life on television. Fred also stops seeing and hearing the KGB men. Fred's emotions are stabilised and he now is able to work a few hours voluntary in a MIND charity shop.

Olanzapine, like Largactil, is non-addictive, but maybe psychologically addictive because of it's ability to calm and sedate the mind; resulting in better mental health. Fred is happy to take the new drug, as he now has greater energy and better relationships with his work colleagues and family. The major impacts of Zyprexa are that it helps increase serotonin levels, thus elevating the patient's mood, and increases the dopamine receptors in the brain. Fred gains due to suppression of depression and anxiety. Although he is prescribed Gaviscon for his vomiting, the Zyprexa drugs are not proven to cause nausea. Fred's oesophagus has been irreversibly damaged and this is more likely to be the cause of his reflux.

Other impacts on Fred are increased appetite and significant weight gain, he is now 20 stone. Fred walks and tends to his garden regularly, but this does not alleviate his obesity. Fred also feels that he is alienated from his environment: it is "unreal." He also feels drowsiness and dizziness at times; common side effects of Zyprexa.

As Lily states there are , " difficulties in passing urine, a lactating of the breasts, sleepiness, tremors, dry mouth and physical stiffness..."(2008) Also, there is a link with Tardive Dyskinesia and Olanzapine. This is a condition where there are facial tics and involuntary body movements.However, these effects are uncommon with Zyprexa and are more typical of the older antipsychotics.

Olanzapine is most commonly used where typical antipsychotics fail, such as Largactil, and where either schizophrenia, schizoaffective disorder and major bipolar disorder are present. However, it should not be used as a sedative for the suicidal. The suicidal may be depressed and not psychotic; Zyprexa is for psychotic disorders, such as hearing or seeing people and objects, that are not present.. Zyprexa is a powerful anti-psychotic and helps stabilise emotions, such as depression, mood swings, extreme fears and suspicious, irrational thoughts and beliefs. It is most effective at dealing with delusions, such as Fred's mistaken belief that Ben Elton wants to invite Fred on to his TV show. Also, hearing and seeing things, like the KGB, that is unreal.

Fred is now accused of violently attacking his new girlfriend and the neighbours decide to report him to the police.

Although, there is no validity to Fred's aggression, he feels persecuted again and develops a fear of people and what they think or feel about him. His social phobia is now much worse and he uses avoidant tactics, such as staying away from shops and pubs, where he may meet strangers and this triggers stress and anxiety.

Q3/e

DIAZEPAM

The benefits for Fred are his fears and anxiety concerning social situations, they are relieved by valium and suppressed, into the unconscious mind. However, his paranoia about being stalked by Ben Elton remains and he continues to be treated by atypical antipsychotic Olanzapine. Fred feels calmer and more relaxed, so much so that he gives up all smoking and alcohol consumption. Fred now feels less threatened by strangers, so he is able to function socially and he now enjoys better relationships with his family. The Diazepam reduces Fred's inhibitions and therefore his social life is extended to organising his self help group, which he enjoys.

Fred finds that his worrisome and negative thoughts are subdued by valium. Fred no longer feels he is being trailed by the KGB, but he still insists that the comedian Elton wants Fred to appear on a new chat show. However, Fred's emotions are now relatively stabilised by valium, Manerix and Zyprexa. There is now only a slight risk of another breakdown and re-admission to inpatient care. As Diazepam effectively stabilises Fred's moods,

He is now able to receive psychotherapy on a one hour, weekly basis. Thus Valium is not a cure for most anxiety states and therefore counselling is recommended for dealing with Fred's underlying fears of victimisation and persecution. Given Fred's medical history of psychosis, the counsellor may need to apply long-term treatment and short-term problem solving or person-centered therapy may be ineffective because of the childhood dynamics influencing his adult behavior: "The Mother Betrayal" of his mother withdrawing love and protection at an early age, rendering Fred vulnerable to feelings of rejection and fear inducing mental illness.

Diazepam medication is mostly for,"…anticonvulsant, hypnotic, sedative and muscle relaxant uses…" It's hypnotic and sedative properties may help Fred keep calm and relaxed, when he feels "harassed" by Ben Elton. There is a danger of addiction and therefore it should be used for a short term and then replaced by another tranquilliser.

In addition, Diazepam impacts on concentration and coordination; it is not suitable for driving or operating machinery. Fred only uses the bus, so he is fairly safe. MIND suggests that there is, "…memory loss and tiredness…" Fred does not wish to remember his painful past, this may cause problems with his talking therapy; the psychotherapist may wish to explore early childhood rejections and punishments that may have a bearing on his present schizoaffective disorder. Fred's tiredness comes mostly as a result of the drug cocktail that he is using, especially the sedating Olanzapine.

Valium also causes restlessness, excitement, aggressiveness and even nervousness, over a long-term period etc. (MIND) This may lead to over-tiredness and unlawful attacks, such as assault. Fred is very law abiding, so he has little to fear from his own anger.

The uses of Diazepam are as typical medication for chronic anxiety, mania accompanying Bipolar Disorder, Schizophrenia where severe fears are present, schizoaffective disorder, where anxiety accompanies depression, epilepsy where convulsions are frequent and as a physical pain reliever. Diazepam works well with most antipsychotics and antidepressants, with no strong interactions. Fred is now calm and happy, apart from thoughts about Ben Elton chasing him, so he can explore the causes of his illness in counselling; he is stabilised. After 6 months in psychotherapy Fred is able to safely cut back his Diazepam and rely on self help techniques, such as controlled breathing and counting to 10, which helps with his anxiety. The uses of meditation,inducing calmness and a quieter mind, together with positive affirmations, naturally complement the tranquilising effects of valium.

The benefits of diazepam are as a powerful tranquilizers and hypnotic. Patients like Fred benefit from a calmer, more relaxed mind and, if taken at night, a good night's sleep. They are primarily effective for those with crippling anxiety and fear. However, long-term use of diazepam carries a great risk of dependency and some nervous reactions. The client may be addicted to the drug and the beneficial effects may diminish over time. Note, as it is addictive - the client may find any withdrawal from valium worse than the underlying anxiety that the drug was prescribed to subdue.

==

4, 1 Describe the principal symptoms of depression

I will give a brief overall description of depression, followed by a description of the Psychological, Physical and Social Symptoms.

The World Health Organisation states that depression may be defined as a "…depressed mood, loss of interest or pleasure, feelings of guilt or low self-worth, disturbed sleep or appetite, low energy and poor concentration…"

Depression is a prolonged low mood or sadness, that can lead to suicide, especially among the young and men in their 50s, who may feel isolated from friends and relations. The depressed symptoms may last weeks or months and effect basic activities in social, occupational and home settings.

The range of depression is on a continuum from the blues to black depressions. The blues is the most common depression and affects most people at some time in their lives. It is characterised by feeling "fed up" and questioning the value of living. The blues is a non-clinical mood and no anti-depressants need be prescribed by doctors.

Next is Grey depression or Reactive depression; usually occurs after an unfortunate event like redundancy. There may be loss of willpower, but no lack of hope. Suicidal thoughts are fleeting and usually resisted. Black depression or endogenous depression is one of little, if any, will power or hope to carry on living and may require hospitalisation in a psychiatric unit. The general feeling is one of emptiness, uselessness and solitude.

Suicidal thoughts are common and with a great loss of energy prevalent; the ability to commit suicide is less than in grey depression, where there is more energy to carry out suicide. White or psychotic depression is apparent when there is a loss of contact with reality, stagnation, and complete abdication of responsibilities. Suicide may be attempted, although there remains little energy to accomplish it. White and Black depressions are uncommon. (B.H.M.A. 1987)

The Psychological Symptoms also include:-

a/ irritability and intolerance of others

b/ lack of enjoyment in previously enjoyable activities.

c/ frightened, anxious or worried.

d/ low self-esteem

e/ difficulty in decision making

f/ self-harm

g/ reduced sex drive

h/ tearfulness, remorse, feelings of "failure" or "misery".

I/ resentful or envious of others achievements

Physical Symptoms also include:-

a/ changes in appetite with weight gain or loss

b/ slow movement or speech

c/ changes in ladies' menstrual cycles

d/elusive aches and pains

Social Symptoms also include:-

a/ social withdrawal from people, a need to "curl up" in bed or "escape" into one's own space.e.g. home.

b/ loneliness or emptiness

c/ reduced work effectiveness, often leading to loss of employment.

d/ difficulties with family relationships due to the ignorance of family members

Q4.2/

Analyse why depression is more common in women than men.

To understand why depression is seemingly more common in women than men, we need to study in detail the characters found in men; which differ from women.

The factors concerning depression in women are:-

a/ women are twice more likely to suffer depression than men.

b/ there are hormonal considerations that belong to women solely, such as after the birth or before the birth of a child; during menopause, miscarriage and during menstruation.

c/ These hormonal factors in women, after the birth of a child in addition may have other social or physical components, such as pressures of work. I.e. the need to supplement the income for the family. In real poverty the baby maybe unwanted due to the extra responsibilities of caring for and providing for the child. Indeed, the mother rejection may lead to depression in the child, as the child grows. The father may be inadequate to provide both emotionally and financially for the new born baby. The father may see child rearing as a "mother's job".

The client may feel "trapped" in this so-called "mother's job" and depressed due to the emotional and financial reliance on the man as the main "breadwinner."

To some extent this has changed with paid maternity leave and greater occupational opportunities of well paid promotion, due to more women progressing to higher levels of education.

There may be inadequate care and support from doctors or midwives, which may prevent the mother from fully recovering mentally and physically. The hormonal, physical and social factors above may combine to cause anxiety and stress in the woman leading to depression.

d/ Women, especially young women, may model themselves on slim and healthy celebrities and other women in advertisements.
The pressure to follow diets, dress accordingly, keep in shape, keep fit etc may lead to eating disorders and depression. The basic feeling is one of "not being good enough." Men are more likely to follow "macho" or "tough" men as role models, for example, soldiers, athletes, authoritarian fathers and teachers.

The factors of depression in men are:-
a/ men may be unwilling to admit to psychological symptoms due to a social stigma that it is "weak" or "unmanly". Instead, men are more likely to complain of physical symptoms. e.g. back pains, stiff muscles, frequent viruses, such as flu etc. This tends to be more common in men than women.

b/ Men are less likely to be diagnosed as depressed by doctors and mainly treated for their physical symptoms only. e.g. beta-blockers for blood and heart related disorders.. Neither is suitable for depression, although beta-blockers have proved helpful in treating anxiety disorders. Women are more willing to admit to suffering from mental ill health than men, as there is little stigma against doing so.

However, younger males, who have experienced exposure to good health education - may be more likely to seek help for depression than older men who have received little or no health education. Mature men sometimes have been taught to keep a "stiff upper lip" and to see showing emotions as weak and "unmanly."

4.2/c

Men more commonly express their anger and aggression outwardly, whereas women are taught to control these strong emotions and unexpressed anger is a frequent cause of depression in women. Females are more likely to appear as helpless and vulnerable, than men, which could prompt the doctor to diagnose depression in women. However, in recent years there has been seen an increase in girls enjoying once male dominated sports, like football, and school subjects, like drama, where both sexes can express their aggressive emotions. Release of anger is often a way of relieving the causes of depression in childhood.

d/

Men are less commonly to receive sympathetic understanding from family and friends, especially from the more conservative minded who tend to say, "pull yourself together" or "snap out of it" to the depressed relation. This maybe due to ignorance of the severity of the illness or a feeling that somehow depression is a "woman's disease." Such insensitivity is shown to women too.

To summarise, women often endure extra family responsibilities,than men, such as the stress of raising a child, leading to depression. However, it is not necessarily true that most women are more prone to depression than men, as given that more women are seeking professional occupations, with paid maternity leave, there is less additional pressure of providing for a family, especially in a woman's younger years. Paternity leave for men, also allows couples to share the responsibilities and stress of parenting. Less stress leading to a reduced manifestation of depression. There is no scientific evidence that genes or the physical makeup of women, may make women more likely to develop depression. Arguably, it is more likely a result of childhood traumas and good health education that play a greater role in rendering men and women more or less susceptible to depression and not an unproven genetic effect. Nurture, not nature, to me is the greater influence in both sexes.

4.3/ Describe the principal aspects of a hypomanic episode

A hypomanic episode can be defined as "...a distinct period of persistently elevated, expansive or irritable mood...significantly different from the usual non-depressed stage...present for at least 4 days..." (DSM-IV)

The main aspects of hypomania are:-

a/ Grandiosity or inflated self esteem, usually where the sufferer feels able to do or perceive things that non-sufferers cannot. e.g. the patient may believe he is one of the most intelligent beings in the universe or the greatest drum player in a rock band.

4.3b/

The hypomanic client has a reduced need of sleep and is probably not too concerned.

c/ More talkative than in a non-manic state. e.g. "nonsense talk", where the patient speaks loudly and incoherently. The speech may have no roots in reality, except fear

d/ Thoughts and ideas are racing and it may be difficult for the listener to keep pace with the client.

e/ More easily distracted. E.g. by noises or bright colours.

f/ Goal directed activities are increased, e.g. the patient may desire to work abroad, although she maybe in a too distressed state to cope with the work.

g/ Excessive involvement in activities that carry a high risk to the client, e.g. rock climbing whilst under the influence of alcohol. This maybe due to tempting fate

The general principles that apply to a hypomanic episode are:-

1/ There are uncharacteristic changes in psychological and physical functioning, e.g. more outgoing and extrovert behaviour, such as dancing all night without any significant breaks. They may be positive aspects, such as feeling confident enough to approach the opposite sex for a date and this maybe uncharacteristic of the client

2/ Changes in mood and functioning that are observable by others, unless the patient is alone at home. These changes may be positive, such as being more sociable at work or antisocial e.g. using offensive language at colleagues.

3/ The hypo-manic episode is arguably not severe enough to impact on social or occupational functioning; as the client is not psychotic, but in extreme cases of mania this may not be the case., e.g. Bipolar Disorder. Hospitalisation or medication is in most cases not recommended for hypo - manic episodes; it may be suitable for Bipolar manic episodes, if the client is psychotic.

However, if the hypo - manic sufferer is a threat to themselves or others; I would argue that a sedative may be prescribed.e.g. diazepam

4/ The episode is not due to substance abuse, alcohol, drugs or side effects of prescribed medication. However, cases of extreme mania have been reported with drugs, such as Amisulpride. The client may become highly extrovert and say or do inappropriate remarks or be suggestively sexual in public e.g. talking openly about sexual fantasies. Counsellors need to be aware of such side effects and not treat them as a worsening of mental illness.

5/ Accompanying episodes of sustained and severe depression are absent and there is therefore no significant swings from very low to high moods, as in Bipolar disorder.

Q4.4/

Describe the requirements for treating a client that has anorexia.

Some or all of the requirements below may apply to an anorexia sufferer.

a/ Severe obsession with weight gain and a great fear of obesity.

b/ Obsessions with calories and fat in food, which may lead to adding weight.

c/ Dramatic change in weight loss, due largely to reducing food intake.

d/ A tendency to hide food or hoard it. Thus avoiding temptations to eat.

e/ Physical changes may lead to anxiety, loneliness or depression.

f/ These physical and psychological changes may result in a lower sex drive.

g/ Indeed, the psychological changes of anxiety and depression may contribute to low self-esteem, inability to be assertive and lack of confidence.

h/ Fear of eating around others, either due to exposing the client's illness or being tempted to consume more than desired.

I/ Mood swings may be present, from depression to mania.

j/ Tiredness, possibly due to lack of adequate nutrition or insomnia.

k/ Food rituals or secretive eating, such as driving long distances to health shops to purchase low calorie oat biscuits and not being seen eating socially.

l/ Self induced vomiting, such as gagging with fingers, laxative and slimming pill abuse to expel unwanted food from the body.

m/ Strict exercise, such as walking over 10 miles a day to keep slim.

n/ Obsession with food preparation and recipe books, as well as avoiding watching food commercials on television. For example, meat cut to remove excess fat, low calorie recipes and resisting temptations to consume chocolates or other high fat foods.

o/ Self denial of severity of the disorder, so as to avoid therapy or treatment by a GP or Psychiatrist.

p/ Hypothermia due to weight and fat loss.

q/ Lanugos or pre-natal body and face hair

r/ Menorrhoea or cessation of menstrual cycles.

Anorexia Nervosa is a serious eating disorder, which often goes untreated due to the secretiveness and unusual physical and psychological symptoms. However, Anorexia may be due to the client feeling they need to have the "perfect" body, such as those depicted in teen magazines and television commercials.

Q4.5/

Describe the principal features of personality disorders

Personality disorder, otherwise known as "character disorder" or "pervasive chronic psychological disorders" is "an accentuation of one or more personality traits…the traits significantly impairs an individual's, social or occupational functioning." (Encyclopaedia Britannica)

A personality trait may be anger that is expressed as aggression, this trait may be seen as on a continuum from mild anger, swearing, to violent aggressions, such as self harm or attacking others This should not be confused with appropriate anger, expressed in an assertive manner at people or things that affront or cause stress to the client e.g. an abusive man in a pub, belittling or demeaning the client..

The main features are:-

a/ Disturbances in self image, e.g. I'm bad, because I have violent thoughts.

b/ Difficulties in relationships, e.g. inability to find, keep or maintain a loving relationship.

c/ A wide range of emotions, which may be inappropriate, e.g. laughing at others misfortune or displaying hostility to a psychiatrist

d/ Misperceptions of self, other people and the world, e.g. feeling inferior or superior to others depending on whom one is conversing with. Other people or the world maybe perceived as inherently hostile to the client: from the withdrawal of love and protection in childhood; exposing the client vulnerable to the dangers of the world.

e/ Poor impulse control or impulsivity, acting on the "moment" without due regard to consequences. e.g. chatting up a stranger whom is with her spouse. Taking cocaine at a party, where other work colleagues or a boss is present!

Such personality traits above combine to form a distinct pattern of behaviour and inner experiences that are more dramatic and differ substantially from what is deemed acceptable in a given culture. I.e. that which is considered "normal."

The patient may be in constant conflict with others in a given culture, such as grieving sorely in public places, except in churches at funerals and crime locations, when in shock or distress after an accident., Grieving or screaming may be frowned upon in Western Europe. However, such expression of crying is arguably acceptable in mostly muslim Eastern cultures, e.g. Syria.

Q4.5/

In other words, I am arguing that many personality disorders are culture bound and what is deemed as a personality disorder in one culture may be seen as "normal" behaviour or experiences in another.

No matter if a client is diagnosed with a personality disorder, it is important to understand that the sufferer is not psychotic in many cases and medication or hospitalisation is generally unnecessary. As Philippe Pinel said, personality disorders is "…insanity without delusions…"
Arguably, insanity is psychotic, as one loses grounding in reality.

Q4.6/
Analyse the conditions associated with a "split personality"
A split personality is often regarded as a client with a "Jeckyl and Hyde" persona, with one extreme personality of all good to another as one of all "bad." Often this "split" is associated with schizophrenia, but I intend to argue that it bears little resemblance to schizophrenia and more to Dissociative Identity Disorder and Multiple Personality Disorder. The schizophrenic is usually deluded but doesn't behave as two or more personalities.

The "split" or splitting referred to above, usually concerns the developmental stage in youth; when a painful, fearful or angry experience is disconnected in the mind from the present. It is a defence against feeling such strong and powerful emotions; hence the "splitting." However, in schizophrenia one maybe aware of hallucinations, such as Professor Nash in "The Beautiful Mind." Schizoids are usually unaware of their split personality.

a/

Dissociative Identity Disorder

D.I.D. can be seen as part of a dissociation continuum, from the milder everyday disassociation through to Post Traumatic Stress Disorder and D.I.D, at the severe stage.

D.I.D. has a distinctive pattern of thinking and relating to the world; people and events are seen as all good or all bad depending on how these factors satisfy or frustrate the sufferer, e.g. as in abuse, the victim sees the perpetrator as all good in childhood but when she is treated by a psychotherapist, an emotional connection is made with the past abuse and the patient re-evaluates the abuser as all bad. However, this "bad" abuser may not help the client break free from the anguish and rage that may follow from the break, "I'm okay, the abuser is not okay."The ability to trust other adults and move away from chaos and unstable relationships is worked upon. The final outcome for an abused client, is for the client to see the wider picture e.g. mental or emotional abusers may be alcoholics or under unbearable stress.

Obviously, in some abuse cases the abuser is knowingly criminal and the abuser as "not okay" is entirely appropriate e.g. sexual abuse.

A patient with D.I.D. has severe amnesia and is not aware of their alter-ego behaviour. Again the amnesia acts as a defence against experiencing or being restimulated by past painful events. The amnesia is part of the "split personality."

b/

Multiple Personality Disorder

The principal "split" with MPD is one of multiple identities or personalities. I.e. egos or alter egos. As with D.I.D. the Multiple Personality Disorder sufferer has memory loss and is largely unaware of the different personality's behaviour. Each personality or "split" has a distinct pattern of perceiving and interacting socially. The other "split" is unaware of this pattern.

The splitting of the personality may be a result of child abuse, poor nurturing by parents or guardians and traumatic stress , e.g. the death of a close relation.

The client with MPD has two or more personality "splits"; the object of the client and the therapist is to help take control of the various "split" perceptions and behaviour.

The "splits" may exhibit themselves in different ways, such as multiple beliefs, manners, attitudes, headaches, paranoia, depersonalisation, anorexia, depression, flashbacks of abuse or trauma, phobias or social anxiety, tearfulness, lack of personal intimacy, avoidance, deep mistrust of adults or fearfulness and hallucinations. MPD is therefore a psychotic "split" disorder.

Multiple Personality Disorder may be then related to other psychiatric illnesses, notably paranoid schizophrenia, eating disorders, Bipolar disorder, However, the schizophrenic doesn't necessarily have a "split" and delusions and hallucinations may be conscious and therefore able to maintain a one, deluded personality, rather than a multiple personality.

However, in Schizophrenia and Bipolar Disorders there is one major personality because the patient is sometimes conscious of their bizarre perceptions and behaviour when unaffected or not deluded. As argued above, some schizophrenics are conscious of their "altered reality.", during the perceptual disorder. "Split Personality" is a misdiagnosis of Schizophrenia and Bipolar Disorders.

Most schizophrenics would not laugh at a funeral or cry at a humorous comment, unlike the client with disassociation from certain feelings whom may do as a defence against a painful experience.

However, the delusions and hallucinations of a schizophrenic may be seen as disassociations of feelings and events. But, some schizophrenics are conscious of their delusions and hallucinations, whilst experiencing them. Therefore dissociation is not present in those clients.

Indeed, many schizophrenics speak openly about child abuse and other painful memories; which the MPD sufferer denies through repression. Further, in therapy the psychotherapist relates to one schizophrenic personality and not as if to several personalities in one, as in MPD sufferers.

Indeed, MIND states , "It's not true that schizophrenia means "split personality" or that someone will swing wildly from being calm to being out of control."

To summarise, the term "split personality" is often used too crudely and although it properly defines the "split" between present conditions and past traumas, as in Disassociation Disorder and Multiple Personality Disorder; it is somewhat inaccurate as a definition of Schizophrenia. However, some aspects of schizophrenia, such as paranoia and hallucinations, are sometimes symptoms of BPD. e.g. where there is an obvious mistrust of the others intentions. But, may not be conscious in MPD sufferers.

Therefore the BPD client has a "split" between the repressed past trauma and the presenting symptoms e.g. inappropriate aggressiveness. The split may be likened to "Jekyll and Hyde", as one healthy man who undergoes a complete transformation into a psychotic. This may not be present in schizophrenia or Bi-polar disorder and is probably not a condition that can be accurately described as a "split personality."

==================================

Q5.1 Explain for whom group therapy is appropriate

I will attempt to clarify who would be helped by group therapy.

Group therapy is ideal for those patients who seek to develop, explore and exercise, inter-personal relations under the guidance of a facilitator, who has the knowledge, wisdom and leadership qualities to maintain a safe, comfortable environment. Where boundaries are set from the beginning, such as sexual contact, thus maintaining the therapeutic relationship.

Group therapy may be in the form of Group Analysis, which may exclude individual issues; as Yalom argues. However Group Analysis, as it builds up, may encourage individuals to become more confident in social situations. Those with social phobias may feel challenged by group work, but it may help to overcome their fears and increase their comfort zones.

Social skills development is at the core of group therapies, whether it is assertiveness for the socially withdrawn, anxious or for those with anger management problem i.e. for those with BPD who have difficulty suppressing their anger and aggression. BPD , depression and phobic sufferers may all gain from groups that promote "mindfulness, relaxation etc". The focus on becoming aware of thinking, feelings and behaviour, gives the client greater control over how they react to stress triggers e.g. divorce or moving home, workplace etc. Individual face-to-face psychotherapy may supplement and govern limitations of the behaviour of clients in group therapy. A code of conduct, if you prefer.

However, some group therapies that have few rules of conduct, such as Co-Counselling International, may encourage the individual to be too introspective and to feel that catharsis, such as storming rage and shaking off fears, is a hedonistic pleasure that will lead to greater joy and love, as a faculty. The dangers of group catharsis is obvious; raging and shaking body and head may induce hormonal and adrenaline chemicals into the client's brain. The client may become addicted to the noradrenalin "buzz"or repeatedly lose one's temper on a regular basis. Greater fear or anger in the brain and displaced from the physical body, may cause outbursts at work that are not tolerated by employers and the "addictive"client is quickly shown the "door."

The counsellor is often left dealing with the effects of cathartic based group therapy. Cathartic work in groups is more safely used for mature, aware and self-disciplined adults only. It is , I argue, highly unsuitable for minors, as they are vulnerable to persuasion into cathartic work. However, children naturally shake when frightened or rage at their parents or siblings. If they are free to do so as children, surely there is little, if any, gain from cathartic work in adult life. Children respect firm and fair boundaries in home and school life, sadly most cathartic groups lack safe boundaries for the vulnerable youth- due to the "non-judgemental" policies of some cathartic groups. Cathartic groups may be unsuitable to the mentally ill or to vulnerable youth. However, catharism in groups may be useful for mature, largely healthy, mindful adults and it is fair to say, that some Co-counselling groups do not admit those dependent on medication, alcohol or even sugar!

Other group therapies include: dance, music and drama nonverbal expressive therapies. Such therapies may be useful for those whom may find it difficult to verbalise traumas, such as sexual, physical or emotional abuse.

The sufferer may find the cathartic nature breaks down patterns of distress. Arguably the relating of traumatic events in childhood, within an expressive verbal group, may prove cathartic too., e.g. shame and guilt may be shared with other group members and release negative emotions. This cathartic therapy may prove useful for Post Traumatic Stress Disorder clients to express the rage and fear beneath depression. Strict codes of conduct are vital to avoid emotional harm.

Group therapy may be beneficial for psychotic adolescents, especially those who maybe overcoming drug or solvent abuse. Where delusions are common the minor may have controlled or "stable delusions" in a "projective group". The adolescent may identify with a fictional character in a film or book and this may prompt a cathartic release of repressed emotions. The projection may be of an important person in their childhood onto a fictional character in the present , e.g. an abusive authoritarian father or teacher. The emotions released may be safely disposed of within the boundaries of the group, where strict boundaries and enlightened leadership is offered.

Although depressed patients may feel worthless in a group due to lack of one-to-one attention, they may find opportunities to express their feelings of worthlessness. A depressed or BPD sufferer may withdraw in a group and so individual psychotherapy or medication may help overcome the desire to isolate oneself.

Finally, schizophrenics may be too out of touch with reality to benefit from group therapy or a form of grounding:, becoming aware of one's environment and being connected to it., The help of a counsellor and medication may help.

Some schizophrenics do benefit from group work, where the client feels safe and accepted and supported, as a "normal" human with problems. A trained professional therapist must be available at all times, to maintain safety and to demonstrate acceptable boundaries, behavior and appropriate interventions e.g. to control aggressive or violent behavior in a few clients who lack self control.

Group therapy is appropriate for a wide range of illnesses and for building social skills, however caution should be shown for those who maybe too withdrawn, depressed, traumatised or out of touch with reality. Such clients may lack "grounding" and their cognitive abilities may be affected, thus the client is unable to grasp new concepts and gain from them, as they may lack conscious attention. The basic rule should be that the group attendee is mentally "present"

Q5.2/

Evaluate the issues around counselling-online

In this answer I will attempt to define the positive and negative factors concerning on-line counselling.

The main benefits of counselling on-line are lack of face-to-face contact between therapist and client, allowing the client to feel safe, anonymous and have more freedom to talk about serious issues facing the client. This "freedom"and safety may not be forth-coming where webcams are used. The client may be less willing to talk openly about issues, such as abuse, in the case of webcams. The client may fear judgements by expressions of the counsellor and withdraw into silence.

The patient may feel intimidated by a face-to-face session with their therapist, especially if the subjects they are talking about concern embarrassing or otherwise very personal subjects, e.g. sexual dysfunction or sex identity. Instant messaging or texts may promote confidentiality but limit the therapeutic tools that can be applied e.g. visual and audio feedback, as on webcams.

So an online encounter is arguably more private, less intrusive, anonymous etc than face-to-face counselling. This anonymity may allow the client to express themselves more freely and thereby release distress, thoughts and emotions. Patients may express themselves without fear of losing confidentiality, unless the therapist's protocol requires personal data, such as name, address, GP's contact number etc..

Clients may also choose online counselling because they live too far from a specialist therapist, e.g. DEBT counsellor for BPD sufferers. The patient may be housebound due to a physical handicap or live in a remote area, e.g. Scottish Highlands and Islands. A "safe distance" exists to maintain the comfort zone of the client, such as those who fear manipulation or abuse. There is also the factor of cost. I.e. the cost of an e-mail is less than a face-to-face treatment. Social media channels, like Skype or the free Viber service may prove inexpensive and the option of messaging is a arguably, a good ice breaker before face-to-face contact.

The disadvantage of "safe distance" counselling is primarily one of feeling, as a client, that one has revealed too much about their personal life, before a genuine rapport and absolute positive regard has been established, in the therapeutic relationship. A "face-to-face" clinical setting may allow for faster growth of rapport and trust between client and therapist.As, arguably, the client has a more detailed picture of tone, facial and bodily expressions. Such detail may be lacking on webcams and the client may have a visual restriction of how the therapist responds.

On balance, this writer feels that online therapy sadly lacks the genuine authenticity of a clinical room setting and where the counsellor can build up rapport, trust and positive regard more easily than online.However, for more inhibited clients- the online service does provide more freedom of limited visibility and clients can often remain anonymous, although this is impractical and may be unethical, as doctors and next of kin may be needed in an emergency. Greater visibility of both the client's and counsellor's body language, posture, tone, stress on words, intonation etc are all more obvious in the face-to-face room setting.

All of these factors provide a more genuine working environment than an online picture, that often lacks clarity and quality. CBT may prove more adaptive to online therapy, than cathartic work which requires more psychodynamic therapy and it is difficult to see any major movement and validate it e.g. where the patient is expected to crawl on the floor in regression therapy. Online CBT or Person- Centered therapy requires little or no psychodynamic work, so the therapist can more easily see the feedback on screen.

Finally, on balance I feel that because of the visual, audio and spatial difficulties with online therapy and it's lack of authenticity - clinical room settings provide a clearer and more observable contact between counsellor and client. Empathic understanding, absolute positive regard for the client and warmth is difficult to convey in online therapy.

Q5.2/

Language.

The client has a greater control over confidential documents, as e-mails act as a record of progression with overcoming a mental disorder. But, this does raise some security problems, such as "hacking" and "identity theft". Personal information may be leaked, possibly into the public arena, e.g. where illegal acts are confessed. This maybe overcome by firewalls, anti-hacking software and personal passwords. The expense of such measures may outweigh the cost-effectiveness of online counselling. Exchanging emails only, as a form of therapy, have obvious limitations of visual and audio clues to the client's state of mind; it is easier for the client to withdraw and limit the responses to the counsellor's queries and observations.

The validation of issues raised by patients is paramount and with some sufferers a "nod and a wink" may build rapport between the client and therapist, providing visual confirmation, especially with trauma based illnesses. Hence, abused clients may learn to trust the counsellor more and this may help a faster recovery, than just online counselling alone. The solution may be found by using webcams, where some physical clues are apparent from the counsellor. Yet, some anonymity is maintained by the client i.e. limited range of visual image by webcams.

Q5.3/

<u>Analyse the types of validation, their importance and the contexts in which each is used</u>

In this answer I will study in detail the types of approval, their importance and situations in which each is used.

Validation, as it applies to the client, is to respect and acknowledge, confirm and reflect on what has been said by the client: validate the thoughts and feelings of what the client is expressing. The counsellor gives absolute positive regard, holding the client and what they say and do, as genuine, important to both parties, and with great empathy and warmth from the therapist.

The important point is to build up the confidence and self esteem of the patient. I.e. to make the patient feel valued and worthy, no matter what she expresses. This applies to all situations in therapy: one-to-one room counselling, telephone counselling, online counselling or group therapy.

There are 5 distinct forms of patient validation. They are:

1/ Mindful Listening

2/ Reflecting and Acknowledging

3/ Clarifying and Summarising

4/ Problem Behaviour in a wider context

5/ Normalization

1/ <u>Mindful Listening</u>

The most important feature of this is complete, undivided attention; without distraction from what is expressed by the patient in therapy. What is important here is that the client feels valued, listened to and respected. This may involve verbal responses, such as saying "yes" or " I understand". Also, non-verbal responses, such as nodding of the head or maintaining eye contact. Audio responses applies to all forms of therapy, except perhaps with on-line counselling where the responses are typed, as messages or emails. If a webcam is used then accompanying audio sound may be utilised.

Non-verbal, physical, responses apply only to face-to-face counselling, group therapy and to a limited extent where webcams are used, I.e. only facial expressions are understood or physical withdrawal by the client to another part of the client's room. Client withdrawal may indicate stress is apparent and the client feeling vulnerable to exposure, by the counsellor's response e.g. when a member of the family or community is discovered, in therapeutic transactions, to be a catalyst of the problems facing the client. Facial clues include displays of disgust, as in relating abuse, and withdrawal may denote depression, stress or anxiety.

However, client withdrawal may be a response to a breach of confidentiality e.g. another member of the client's family entering the room, where the patient is located, during an on-line session.

2/ Reflecting and Acknowledging

The therapist reflects back what in essence what the patient has said, by repetition, using the therapist's own language, I.e. the therapist's own vocabulary and avoiding repeating the client word for word. Simply to show understanding of what the patient says and feels by feedback; showing concern, empathy and genuine compassion for the client's problems, concerns and disorders. The therapist should, by reflecting, acknowledge the worth and value of what the patient is conveying. This should apply even in situations where the therapist fundamentally disagrees with what has been said by the patient.

By reflecting the counsellor is really showing that the patient is taken seriously and with acknowledgment, the counsellor is demonstrating the importance of what is expressed by clients. No matter what.

 In reflection, a client may say that, " I feel ashamed in front of my parents that I am gorging myself on junk food and that I feel so bad that I just want to beat myself up." The therapist may reply," So you feel guilty about overeating and are you seeking to punish yourself through self harm because you feel so bad. Is that right? " The client confirms the analysis by nodding in agreement.The counselor may continue by saying, "So does it seem that beating yourself up is a self punishment, that you do by self-harm? Is this right?"

The therapist has , in his own words, reflected back what has already been said by the client and acknowledged the feelings of the patient. The conversation has been clarified by the counsellor's prudent analysis and the client's response to the therapist.

Reflection is a vital tool in any type of counselling, but may be difficult to convey in an e-mail because there is no instant response. Acknowledgement is equally important but may prove problematic in on-line counselling, except where more direct conversation takes place, e.g. instant messaging and by webcam.

3/ Clarifying and Summarising

Clarifying is simply making clear what the client is trying to convey and therefore show understanding of what has been said. The therapist needs to know and be clear in his mind what is actually being said and felt by the patient. The counsellor does this by asking direct questions, such as " Am I correct in understanding that you think about suicide every day?" Thought provoking questions gives greater clarity, as the patient then has to think more carefully as to what the counsellor is actually attempting to elucidate. Clarifying applies to all types of counselling, as long as there exists adequate time to think freely and express. Sessions of 50 to 60 minutes are usually sufficient, with 5 to 10 minutes of summarising, at the end of each session.

In Summarising the patient ensures she is completely understood by asking the therapist questions and that she is not being misunderstood. The client is able to correct any misconceptions by the counsellor. The summary is vital for ensuring that all major issues or other relevant details are not omitted e.g. all the main factors and people in a traumatic event, such as a car accident. Summarising is important if the patient is to be valued and understood, failure to do so may lead to a lack of trust in the therapist and a misdiagnoses of the client's disorder.

Summarising should be used in all kinds of psychotherapy, especially in groups where there is too often, too little time for clients questions and feedback.

4/ Problem Behaviour

The important point here is to put problem behaviour in a wider context, in order to avoid patients from self harm, being aggressive or offensive, or suicidal. The problem behaviour is not ignored but placed in context. For example, a client may have sworn at her child but the therapist replies by saying , "Yes, you did swear at your son, but you had corrected him at least a dozen times about breaking the computer console and yet he continued to do it."

The therapist can validate that the situation didn't escalate into violence and that the client's behaviour is justifiable and "normal". The importance of this example: no violence and the context was the challenging behaviour of the son.

5./ Normalization

The counsellor acknowledges the client's feelings and reactions as normal or "legitimate"(validation). A good example is one where the client invites 21 friends to a party and only 2 turn up. The client feels rejected and angry at her friends and tells the counsellor. The therapist replies by saying, " Yes, I would feel just like you if my best friends failed to attend a party that I had spent hours preparing for, and so would most people".

The normalization is that the therapist perceives the client's feelings as valid. This encourages the patient to perceive her anger as normal and the context is the patient's reaction to the ignorance or indifference of her friends not attending the party. The client sees her emotions as normal, justified, and approved by her therapist. (The Importance.)

Q5.4/

Analyse the issues around managing out of session contact with clients

I will study in detail the positive and negative factors concerning the management of therapist-client relations out of sessions.

It is important to set boundaries from the outset of counselling, to prevent the breakdown of good therapeutic practice, between therapist and client. Indeed, it may be necessary to draw up a verbal or written contract, such as respecting the privacy and free time of the counsellor. Then, the patient knows the limits of contact with her counsellor and avoids "fuzzy" boundaries, which are unclear and cause further distress to the client, such as physical attraction.

It should be made clear that the patient generally should not contact the therapist out of hours, unless it is vital or concerns the patient's well being, such as self harm or feelings of suicide. The therapist should direct the client to a helpline, such as Samaritans or recommend she seeks help from a psychiatrist or GP, if the suicidal threat to life is imminent. Indeed, the counsellor may, if the client is in immediate danger, strongly suggest that the client presents herself to the nearest NHS Casualty Department. Again, it is important that the ethical code of conduct of the counsellor's professional body is adhered to e.g. the BACP.

The counsellor should avoid telling the client that out of session contact is "intrusive" and "a disturbance". This language would be disturbing to a client seeking immediate help for self harm or suicidal feelings, and may worsen the condition of the patient. Instead the counsellor may seek to explain the immediate interruption to his free time e.g. "I understand that you are depressed and feeling unwell but I have visitors and we are about to dine. Please call the Samaritans or, if you are able, wait to our next appointment. Take care and see you soon." Empathy, warmth and understanding is needed in a life-threatening situation. Choice and tone of words are vital, to avoid further stress to an already ill client. Although, in less urgent cases, such as after a client has had a row with her boyfriend and no threat to her life is apparent, in speech or tone, the rules of the therapist's governing body should be strictly adhered to. Family life, leisure activities and other commitments may be impacted upon, if the code of conduct is not applied.

However, many therapists have different rules of conduct, than that of a professional body, like the BACP. It is a delicate issue and it is important that the out of sessions contact rules are acknowledged by the patient and made valid, by sensitive explanation. The psychotherapist's intuition, knowledge and understanding of his clients is paramount in cases of out of session contact.

Setting contracts or boundaries is important if client dependency upon the therapist is to be avoided. Without boundaries the patient may feel that the counsellor is always there for her and can call at anytime, with any problems, such as when feeling depressed or simply feeling lonely.
Often the patient has few close friends, confidants or interested relations who are warm and empathic. This is understandable and reasonable. The counsellor may suggest befriending by a Samaritan. Samaritans are free to call or visit and most are non-judgemental. However, Samaritans are not counsellors and may experience difficulty in understanding and helping someone with a psychotic disorder, such as schizophrenia or Bipolar Disorder.

In addition to the Samaritans,,the therapist may recommend to the patient attending a day hospital, even a communal retreat that could help the client feel less isolated, depressed and therefore release pressure on the counsellor.

The safe boundaries concerning out of session contact include sexual relationships, business ventures, lending money, or sharing leisure times together, such as drinking alcohol or having meals together. Failure of a counsellor to comply to these codes of conduct may lead to disciplinary sanctions and even expulsion by the psychotherapist's professional body.

Many of the above issues are unethical and represent bad practice, by the therapist, as they lead to familiarisation and the disruption of the therapeutic treatment, such as maintaining professional objectivity and impartial advice. Indeed, the client may feel angry that the therapist is suggesting ideas that would not normally be suggested by a friend, e.g. the client's mother evoked guilt in sexual matters, such as showing disapproval of masturbation in the client's youth Also, the patient may have lacked sex education at home or at school. Parental or teacher's disapproval may cause unnecessary shame and guilt in the client, from an early age.

The client may feel her privacy has been invaded; withdraw and lose trust in the counsellor. Arguably, masturbation guilt maybe the root of the client's sexual guilt or identity. In this case, the therapist should ask kindly if the client feels ready to explore such sensitive subjects. This is arguably not an issue that can be dealt with easily on the phone, online, or by text and should be only discussed in face to face sessions and not in out of session encounters. Masturbation is rarely an issue of immediate danger to the client, except possibly in cases of sexual abuse.

Clearly the safe boundaries of the client-therapist relationship must be maintained to avoid a breakdown of trust and impartiality. However, there are times when out of session contact is applicable to the therapeutic relationship, e.g. when notice has to be given, by the patient, for the patient's holiday leave, sickness or other commitments, such as appointments with a psychiatrist. Equally the therapist may need to notify in advance if he is sick, taking a vacation, a family wedding or simply to notify change of session times, location of room etc. The out of session contact, usually by phone, maybe unavoidable by therapist or client when changes to appointments are necessary. The main consideration is one of safe and clear boundaries in all cases. Some professionals charge fees, even if 24 or 48 hours notice is given by the client of lateness or cancellation. The client may have a very good reason for missing an appointment with her therapist and a fee, however small, may be seen as a punishment or rejection by the client. Suicidal depression or severe self harm are cases where the psychotherapist would be wise to display some flexibility..

Q5.5/ Analyse the implications of working within an ethical and legal framework

I will study in detail what follows from working within moral standards of practice and within the law.

Working ethically

The therapist agrees to work within a set code of ethics or standards and to abide by them. These set standards cover all aspects of a counsellor's practice but are not necessarily bound by law.

The British Association of Art Therapists have a code of ethics which the therapist should follow:

1/ maintain registration of a counselling or non-verbal association.

2/ must comply with Principles of Professional Practice and its guidelines.

3/ undertake regular supervision from a qualified supervisor.

4/ undertake continuing professional development (CPD)

Maintaining registration of a counselling association means not only keeping up with annual fees but also following their own code of ethics.

These standards or ethical code must not be contravened.

Termination of membership may follow if the counsellor has committed a criminal act or has been suspended or dismissed by another health body, e.g. a local Mental Health NHS Trust.

However, the criminal act may be minor and somewhat unrelated to counselling, such as driving 40 mph in a 30 mph speed limit zone or being dismissed maybe due to difference of analysis that conforms to more mindful or de-repressed mind set than conventional approaches, like CBT.

Confidentiality

Perhaps the most important part of good counselling practice is maintaining confidentiality, especially where the patient is concerned. It is vital for trust and safety for both the therapist and client. However, confidentiality may be broken if the client or a minor is at risk. In these cases the therapist may contact the psychiatric or police services, in line with the governing body's agreed framework.

1/ The counsellor holds in confidence verbal and nonverbal information gained from his patient.

2/ The disclosure of client's information is met by the patient's agreement.

3/ Disclosure is compulsory if the law demands it, e.g. Mental Health Act

4/ The protection of the client is paramount but if non-disclosure affects the safety of the patient, therapist, psychiatrist, community nurse or any other member of the public, then disclosure is usually necessary. However, the patient should be consulted before any action is taken.

5/ Confidentiality also applies to child protection and the care of vulnerable adults, I.e. those at risk of abuse or exploitation. Where therapy is at risk or young people are placed in a vulnerable situation, than non- disclosure is recommended, e.g. to parents, carers, guardians etc.

Accountability and consistency of care

1/ To be aware of the current laws and changes that affect the counsellor's practice, e.g. mental health acts and child protection acts

2/ When "ending" therapy either at the client's request or by the decision of the therapist alternative therapy, treatment or help lines should be offered. Ending of therapy should avoid causing unlawful acts, e.g. damage to property or child abuse. So, possible effects need to be discussed with health professionals

.

Clinical Judgement

1/ There should be no impairment of judgement by the therapist, e.g. due to bias, prejudice, racism, sexism, etc. Sexual abuse is a crime and a certain bias to the law is acceptable.

2/ Also further impairment by drugs or alcohol are prohibited. This mostly applies to mind altering drugs, such as taking cannabis but some prescribed medication for mental health may be acceptable. This should depend on the ability to function normally in a clinical setting and arguably should not be dependent on the exact medication e.g. diazepam

3/ No therapist should work where mental or physical illness affects their judgement

If the mental or physical illness is relieved by the drugs, then arguably this should not be an ethical requirement.

4/ All therapists should seek assistance from a professional, such as a GP, where health is affecting their practice and by a supervisor, where matters of conflict, such as projection or transference or methodology is harming the therapeutic relationship. Morally, there should not be prejudice or bias based on the mental health of high functioning counsellors.

5/ No "Dual Relationships" whereby there is a clinical impairment due to a friendship, affair, business or other distinct relationship, other than that of patient-therapist relationship within the safe boundaries of a purely therapeutic one. However, sexual attraction between both counsellor and client is unavoidable but one must be mindful of such biological issues.

Records

Records of client's attendance, notes of client's verbal and nonverbal expressions and information in sessions, should not be shared with anyone except with the client, supervisor and agencies required by law,e.g. a criminal court. Again within the current laws of the clients or counsellors jurisdiction. I.e. in cases of violent crime or crime against property; the law enforcers may need to know the movements and whereabouts of suspected criminals

The records should be safely kept in a book, diary, folder, on tape or computer disc and stored away from other patients, parents, guardians, carers etc. These records are highly confidential and should be destroyed, after therapy has closed and after consultation with the clients concerned. Again, the police may need such evidence or verbal disclosures for supporting a criminal investigation. E.g. a computer may be taken away, by the police, for investigating downloads of illegal sexual images. However, the police must have approval by the criminal courts.

Financial

In private practice the fees payable by patients or guardians should be completely honest, genuine and transparent, e.g. no hidden costs, such as additional charges for couples or work at weekends. The fees payable by the patient should be easily understood and any alterations should be given with reasonable notice to the client e.g. such as a month's notice.
In the case where the patient is incapable of affording the new fees and alternative treatment may be offered elsewhere. No fees for referrals made by other health authorities or professionals; made payable by the client or agency. The clinical fees and how often they are payable, e.g. once a week, should be stated at the outset of therapy, together with payment methods, such as cash.

The counsellor morally needs to be sensitive to the income status of the client and, if possible, there is a moral case for offering discounts or a sliding scale based on the client's personal status. Some therapists, for good reasons, don't offer any discounted sessions and with professional bodies, like the BACP, there is no ethical or legal demand for such therapists to do so. This is a sensitive issue for both clients and counsellors in times of financial hardship. Ultimately, it is down to the good sense of the counsellor alone.

Session frequency and the session duration, such as once a week for 12 weeks or indefinitely, and whether there is any flexibility, should be made clear from the outset. Charges for cancellations, e.g. client's sickness, or holidays should be transparent.Failure to do so creates fuzzy boundaries and possible misunderstandings, that may lead to arguments between the therapist and the client. The implications of this may cause stress to both parties and a breakdown of the professional relationship e.g. the client may terminate the sessions completely and avoid further analysis, due to the client's mistrust of the counsellor.

Private Practice

Sometimes therapists claim to have qualifications they do not possess, often to invite higher paying clients. The patient should always ask the therapist for proof of qualifications to avoid being manipulated and deceived. Therapists should never claim to have qualifications or work experience, such as voluntary helpline work with the Samaritans, that they did not undergo. It is immoral, in my opinion, and could lead to disciplinary procedures by the counsellor's professional body.

The later discovery, perhaps in discussions, by the patient, that she is being deceived may allow the client to judge the counsellor as untrustworthy and project her experience of mistrust onto some or all therapists. The psychotherapist may have his career terminated early and find great difficulty in finding work that involves a great deal of trust.

Therefore, the type of counselling offered should match that of the therapist's training, qualifications and experience, e.g. DBT for BPD sufferers; if qualified or experienced in that field. Again, the counsellor may have worked with clients whom have a personality disorder on another therapeutic approach, e.g. Gestalt, and his awareness and mindfulness may be sufficient to identify with and have knowledge and empathy of the client and her condition.

The counsellor should always ask the permission of the client before consulting their GP, Psychiatrist, CPN, for details of medical history or medication. Much of this information is confidential and in most cases the medical history and other health issues will be provided by the client, in the sessions.

Further, the police may need to approach the client's doctor for disclosure under laws of child abuse. This confidential information, of what the client has disclosed in good faith, is no longer bound by the ethics of the doctor's Hippocratic Oath. The implications of this are far ranging, as abusers are now more likely to tell lies and go undetected by the law enforcers. Arguably, some sexual predators may fail to get the appropriate treatment e.g. counselling or anti-arousal drugs.

To protect the counsellor from unlawful accusations or defamatory remarks, the therapist should have Indemnity Professional Insurance. It is also within the law to apply to the Data Protection Agency, if data concerning the patient is kept on a computer at home.

Although, records and files of sessions are privy to the police, if a warrant is issued by a local magistrate.

Treatment

 1/ "A life worth living" may be the main goal for the patient seeking therapy and the counsellor should set clinical standards to achieve this, reflecting the needs and strengths of the patient. Much of this will depend on the awareness by the client of her illness, limitations and potential.

It would be fairly pointless for the therapist to concentrate on mood related illnesses and their impact on thoughts, if the client is unaware of her moods. Likewise suggesting a rubber band for a BPD client who is suicidal may be inappropriate, given the violence and rage which may need a stronger substitute, e.g. pillows or a mattress to beat and pound. However, a person focused trained therapist or cognitive therapist may morally disagree with, or have no awareness, of cathartic work and the underlying rage may go untreated.

So, it is imperative that the counsellor reviews, adapts and revises the client's treatment frequently. Thus avoiding non-productive forms of therapy and providing the safety and relevant support towards healthy functioning of the patient. Keeping therapy within an ethical code and a legal framework will help maintain the highest possible standards of care, emotional growth and safe boundaries for the client to explore.

However, the patient may experience lack of trust in the counsellor and untold stress due to the invasive powers of the State. New laws may protect the innocent but may seriously affect the trust in what is revealed to the counsellor in good faith.

To conclude, it seems that ethics applied by the counsellor are not always conducive to the full adherence to the legal framework e.g. maintaining confidentiality and protecting those at risk.

Q5.6/

Evaluate the importance and implications of routine evaluation of the counsellor's own practice.

I will answer what is important about supervision of the therapist and his practice, and the effects concerning supervision.

The main task of supervision is to ensure the effectiveness of the therapeutic relationship between the therapist and her client.

To see that standards of therapy are being maintained and that the counsellor's practice is relevant and ethical, regarding the patient's treatment.

The counsellor should raise any questions or problems that are applicable to the therapeutic relationship. E.g. anger management of the patient. Also, confidential notes should be discussed with the supervisor. Provide feedback on how a client is progressing and what goals and techniques are being used, e.g. " a life worth living". CBT, and DBT for BPD sufferers.

The supervisor should "widen the horizons" of the therapist by encouraging a greater understanding of illnesses, such as schizophrenia, and encourage new tools of analysis, e.g. CBT. The therapist and supervisor should arrange to exchange ideas and feedback, at least once a month to discuss the ongoing therapeutic relationship between patient and counsellor. What is discussed in supervision should be totally confidential and aim towards the safety of the therapist and client, e.g., self harm prevention and preventing violence towards the counsellor. In situations where there is a high risk of the client causing damage to herself or others, the supervisor may offer advice, such as police or psychiatric care, to further aid the distressed client. Confidentiality may need to be broken, whereupon outside agencies, like social services, feel a legal requirement to ascertain the facts..

Transference

In supervision, the supervisor should aim to resolve transference of an image that a client may project onto a therapist that does not befit the character or behaviour of the counsellor ,e.g. a patient sees the therapist as a father figure who is authoritarian and sadistic and is unhelpful on all matters. Indeed, this may be a unhelpful relationship in the practice, as the client may fear exploring difficult issues with the "Daddy" counsellor,e.g. psycho-sexual problems or neuroses.

However, if the projected image changes to bigoted father, then the client may feel shame and guilt about sexual matters.

The supervisor's role is therefore one of bringing to the attention of the counsellor the unconscious feelings the client may hold about the counsellor.

Only when the unconscious allegiances become conscious can the negative aspects be challenged,e.g. a brutal father was unkind becomes the "unkind" therapist. Supervision must act on transference if objectivity and the client's safety is to be upheld. This is most urgent as the effects of negative projections onto the therapist may lead to a breakdown of trust. Thus, the patient may terminate the counselling sessions before , "a life worth living", has been established."

Countertransference

One of the greatest challenges facing the supervisor and therapist is the transference of unconscious feelings from the counsellor to the client. The therapeutic relationship may be impaired and the objectivity of the counsellor undermined, if countertransference is not addressed, e.g. if a therapist projects onto his patient an authoritarian and abusive father, the counsellor may fear challenging the rigid patterns of thinking and behaviour of the "Daddy" schizophrenic.The client or counsellor will neither progress until the supervisor "unlocks" the counter-transference by the therapist. This may take the form of recognising the differences in identity between the projected patient and the real father or by de-repression, e.g., dream analysis, fantasy work, co-counselling etc.

Projection (projective identification)

The supervisor's role is also to unlock projections by therapist or client, I.e. emotions, thoughts and beliefs, such as a patient believing that all bald men are abusive and therefore she cannot trust the "abusive" counsellor, who is bald. The supervisor may recommend that the counsellor asks the client what is similar and what is different about the therapist compared to the patient's experience of bald men. Bald-headed men, like my father were mentally cruel and dismissive of my academic success at school. However, under Socratic questioning, the client may reveal that a kind, bald-headed teacher was encouraging and took a positive attitude of the clients educational attainment.

The projetcion can be a positive one too, such as all elderly women are happy and good listeners, due to the client's experience of her own, well balanced, Grandmother.It is important that that the client is able to discern the difference from a nurturing identity and a destructive identity i.e. not all mature women are kind or cruel. The implications of perceiving all men or women as positive or negative influences, can lead to traumas in the future, when the client is treated negatively by an opposite character e.g. the bald, "kind" man kills her pet because he is a psychopath. An extreme example and less traumatic incidents are more common e.g. projected identification of the client perceiving the therapist as sexually attractive because of desiring the qualities of her father. Father as handsome, kind, talented etc.

However, if the therapist projects onto her client negative feelings, then the trust, objectivity and empathy may be lost, e.g. a counsellor who has had a negative experience with a violent schizophrenic may project a belief that her next schizophrenic patient is also dangerous, where this is not necessarily the case.Clearly this belief is unethical and the supervisor needs to evaluate whether the therapist is out of his depth and possibly encourage further training.

Dependency

The supervisor should regularly evaluate whether boundaries are well defined and not "fuzzy". I.e. clarity between the possibilities and limitations of therapy, such as non-dependency on the counsellor. Indeed, the counsellor should feel free to talk through any form of dependency that is developing in the therapeutic relationship.

The most common form of dependency is where the client reacts to the therapist as if she is good Mother or good father. This reaction of the patient is ultimately disabling, as the dependency encourages the client to rely on the counsellor for decision making and thereby lessens the patient's own ability to reach her own decisions and act on her own wisdom and common sense. However, the parent(s) may have given the client a great deal of freedom over important decision making and allowed her to rely on her own judgements. Autonomous behavior by the patient is encouraged in the humanistic and other models of psychotherapy, and is one of the stated outcomes of the counselling relationship.

This kind of dependency can be challenged by the supervisor by asking the supervisee if she is acting as a good parental figure who can deal with all of the client's problems, neurosis or psychosis. Much of the therapist's behaviour towards the client will be unconscious and de-repression tools may be essential, e.g., intensive counselling by the supervisor, such as cathartic work.

The importance of routine evaluation is to ensure boundaries are kept to and the effectiveness of the therapeutic relationship is maintained. The implications of this are that frequent observation by a qualified supervisor is ongoing and that the safety and highest standards of ethical practice are upheld. The effects on the counsellor's own practice are that the ethical and legal code of the therapist's professional body are adhered to and a highly professional counselling relationship are abided by, where good practice and desired outcomes are achieved.

Q 5.7/

Evaluate the importance of maintaining sound administrative systems.

I will find the value in the importance of having good management in the therapist's practice.

An Agreement

The agreement or contract at the beginning of therapy is important, as it lays down what is expected from the therapist and client. It should be simple and easily understood. It should stress the frequency and duration of sessions.

For example, 50 minutes every week, for 10 weeks. It is important to realise that the session belongs to the client, as it is they who volunteer information and are the payees.

Fees for the session are normally collected at the beginning or at the end of the hour. The therapist should state before therapy commences the cost and how much notice is required if the counsellor changes the fees. Honesty and clarity is important to avoid disputes and misunderstandings. There should be a cash box and an accounts book. Spare change should be kept in the box and a written credit entry of the fees paid by the patient, in the accounts book. The client should not have to pay for several weeks fees or the counsellor forced to wait weeks until the patient has the correct dues. Unless, there are special circumstances, such as long-term illness that prevents the client from paying her dues. Also, plenty of spare change of notes and coins will prevent any inconvenience, at the time of payment. Delayed fees should be discussed at the outset of therapy to avoid arguments and mistrust. This is important for good administration and vital trust between parties, without it the counselling relationship may end.

Further inconvenience may occur where the patient does not give notice of a cancellation. Usually the patient will have to pay for any missed appointment regardless of notice or circumstances. However, some therapists may prioritise those clients struggling with economic hardship and waive cancellation charges or even reduce their fees.
The therapist should be consistent about accepting low fees, as it may cause a precedence. Also, it may be difficult for the counsellor to increase the fees at a later date.

It is important that sufficient time is given for cancellations and any changes, such as the ending of therapy. If the therapist is ill equipped to continue with a particular patient, then the counsellor should offer some alternative help, e.g. an NHS psychologist or a psychiatrist.

It is important that the patient does not feel abandoned or rejected by "endings" and the termination of therapy should be well planned. In some cases the voluntary or self help sector is inadequate for clients with severe distress patterns, e.g. schizophrenia or suicidal depression. And it is important that the client obtains the optimum help from health professionals, whom are specialists in the client's scope of disorder. E.g. a behavioral therapist for a patient with borderline personality disorder

It is important to liaise not only with the patient, but also the parents, partners, guardians and health professionals. They may have a wider experience of the

client's behaviour and needs, thereby creating greater input into the patient's

treatment. Flexibility is paramount here if the client is to receive fair and consistent therapy and that does require good organisation by the counsellor.

The Setting

Good management is also about providing the proper environment for the therapeutic relationship, to maximise comfort and healing. The client should be sitting in a relaxed position in an armchair that is level with the therapist's chair.

This is to avoid a feeling of inferiority or being dominated by the counsellor, which may increase distress patterns and inhibit what the patient says. The room should be brightly coloured with pleasant framed pictures, e.g. of animals, the sea, woodlands, etc. The lighting should be bright, but not distracting. The room should be heated and warm in the cold Winter but fresh air and a fan may help keep the client comfortable in the hot Summer months. Liquids should be available for the patient, preferably hot and cold drinks, e.g. soothing camomile or decaffeinated tea for anxious patients. Caffeine drinks should be avoided, as they stimulate adrenalin, creating more anxiety in the client. Pillows or cushions placed near the client are important for any cathartic release of anger or grief. Thus keeping the patient and counsellor safe from violence.

Ideally there should be no noisy distractions from inside or outside the therapy room. Too much noise may cause the client to lose focus on important issues. If there is a distracting noise from outdoors, such as drills or heavy traffic, the counsellor may ask the client if she would prefer the windows closed. Also, the client may feel inhibited by the voices of staff or other clients outside the therapy room. The counsellor may need to ask the "loud" spoken people to move politely away from the therapist's door. This particularly applies to those clients who have high anxiety or paranoid tendencies.

A handshake at the end of the session may be okay, except where the client has intimacy problems, e.g. OCD or a victim of abuse. A polite goodbye and reassuring compliments, e.g. enjoy your week ahead etc., apply to telephone counselling too. During and at the end of sessions tissues may be offered, for patients in grief or distress.

Telephone Counselling

The counsellor should read her notes thoroughly concerning the patient's disorder and have an organised plan for the usual hour. The hourly sessions should include 5-10 minutes for feedback and comments by the therapist and client. The counsellor may ask, "Do you feel I have been on your side, fighting for you?" This is good practice as the client is empowered to comment directly on the usefulness of the therapist's analytical approach and determine if the patient wishes to continue with the counsellor or not. A non-vocal client may be prompted to open-up by such a direct question by the counsellor and feel more inclined to speak in future sessions.

The counsellor should withhold her phone number to maintain privacy and avoid the client calling her out of sessions. Thus avoiding the stress of habitual calling by the patient. Most telephone companies provide witheld number facilities and a separate cell phone for counselling may also be used. Thus maintaining a division between private friend and family calls and the sessional calls.

A free call service, provided by telephone servers, is an attractive option and ensures the client is called at the beginning of sessions. There are packages, provided by the phone operator, that have inclusive minutes and that enable the therapist to call the client's cell phone. This is particularly helpful where the client needs to speak candidly, away from family members.

The counsellor must allow for pauses and long silences by the patient, especially after thought provoking interventions. As the patient has to think in a distressed state of mind and therefore needs time to think through a suitable answer. A variety of techniques should be employed depending on the answers given by the patient. Patently it is obvious that if CBT is not proving results then important time and money, if applicable, is being wasted. Therefore, arguably the best approach is an integrated one, where the counsellor draws on a wide range of analytical tools. The counsellor may keep a record of the most appropriate techniques for different conditions. Good management means revising and reading up on new or alternative skills of therapeutic interventions. Also, regular supervision and widening knowledge of modern issues, approaches and skills through CPD.

Confidentiality and notes

The therapist needs to keep records of attendance, notes of what was said and done in the sessions by therapist and client; short words taken during sessions too. To ensure good administration and avoidance of confusion over a mass of irrelevant or less important notes; it is simpler and more lucid, if the notes are one or two sentences of abbreviated keywords.

It is important that the supervisor is made aware of these notes and this may be achieved by e-mailing the notes and discussing their content at supervisory times. Although, emails are vulnerable to cyber crime and one may argue that the notes should be hand written and handed to the supervisor at the appropriate time. Without these notes the supervisor has no knowledge of how well a therapist is performing and if the client is progressing. Good organisation means the notes are coded and brief, so as to keep them private. This applies particularly to emails.

The clinical notes must be kept in a secure folder or on a computer with a password. Good management means securing patient's notes and ensuring that confidentiality is upheld. Good management may mean locking the client's files in a cabinet or by purchasing anti-virus software, if the notes are kept on a PC. Ideally the notes should be written up soon after the end of a session, whilst the details are fresh in the counsellor's mind, as a good memory cannot be relied upon and the significance of what took place may alter over time. The 10 minutes at the end of the session are the best time to reflect and write notes on what has just taken place. Where there are more complicated and detailed admissions by the client; notes need to be taken unobtrusively during the client's sessions.

A sound administrative system is important if accuracy, understandable procedures, clarity, honesty, reliable reflection, adequate supervision and confidentiality is in place to foster a progressive therapeutic relationship between therapist and client. Arguably the best administrative systems are one where the client is consulted, especially on note taking, and the notes are brief and do not intrude on the client's or counsellor's concentration: keep it concise..

===

ASSIGNMENT 6

_____

Q.1 Analyse why people may consider taking their own life

I will study in detail why people may think about taking their own life.

Suicide is the intentional act to end one's life and usually because of unbearable emotional or physical pain. Suicidal attempts may be a cry for help, punishment of parents and friends, a desire to test fate or even an attempt to be a martyr for a political cause e.g. for greater freedom like in the Suffragette movement. The reasons why a person may consider suicide is varied and depends on each individual's circumstances. A patient may feel that there are no other options available to them or maybe so distressed that they cannot reason their way out of depression and suicidal ideation.

It is the therapist's task to offer positive, realistic alternatives to suicide and to study the emotional dynamics behind the need to take one's life e.g. bullying and abuse by a parent or school adolescents.It is important to consider why some children and young people, between the age of 11 and 25 years, attempt suicide. Some factors are exam stress, the shame of having acne, obesity, conforming to the ideal looks - imposed by images in advertising and poor role models e.g. millionaire soccer players and fashion models. As young people grow older, so does the risk of suicide.

Over 50% of those attempting suicide have also self-harmed and counsellors need to be sensitive to the risk of suicide by young people who have self-harmed. Compassion, empathy, non-judgemental attitudes and a unshockable response are the key points in handling the suicidal young.

Most people who consider taking their lives are depressed and not just fed up or feeling the blues. Some 90% of those who consider suicide are depressed. This may also apply to "heroic" suicides, such as in the case of IRA hunger strikers. The conditions of prisons may be so harsh that the inmate may consider suicide, in the form of starvation to death.
..
Most people have some stressful or traumatic events in their lives and are able to find ways of coping but a suicidal client may have a series of traumatic events that seem endless and inescapable. The suicidal feel they are trapped by their negative experiences and may wish to end a pattern of trauma or use attempted suicide as a call for help. They may feel that no one cares about their plight and they feel hopeless, helpless and without alternatives to suicide.

Some suicidal patients may wish to punish themselves or others who they feel have betrayed or given up on them. A loss of a close partner or the death of a relative may trigger suicidal ideation. The suicidal may feel that they cannot continue living without the lost partner or relative.

Suicide is most common in adults, over 50, who may have lost many friends or relatives. Loneliness and a feeling of uselessness is common to the young and old, especially if they are unemployed.

Everyone needs to feel loved and valued by friends and family. A feeling of emptiness and creeping worthlessness may trigger one to consider suicide. A suicidal client may feel both hopeless and helpless.

It is vital that the counsellor recognises the early symptoms of a suicidal patient: depression, acting in an unusual way e.g. making a Will or being over tidy in her own home and social withdrawal from others.

By committing suicide it may seem a suitable punishment for relations who don't seem to care about their suicidal state and relieve any guilt or pain the client feels e.g. feeling responsible for the parent(s) withdrawal of love and nurturing in early childhood. The therapist may find the cause of the suicidal client's guilt is revealed by asking the client, "Have you felt this guilt before and what was happening at the time?"

Suicidal feelings are often rooted in childhood traumas, like the withdrawal of love and nurturing or emotional, physical or sexual abuse. There maybe much anger and grief in the client, that has long been suppressed and turned inwards, as in the case of suicidal attempts or self harm.

Loss of a career or professional standing may induce suicidal thoughts, especially if the job was emotionally rewarding and seen as a vocation. Take the example of a school teacher who has spent years in a career that she loves and has found vocational fulfillment. Suddenly, the bureaucratic paperwork and testing of the kids puts her under great stress. She begins to underperform, takes time off work and is made redundant. The situation seems hopeless with high unemployment and little money to pay for rent and food. The teacher becomes suicidal and is referred to a counsellor.

Although there maybe many teaching vacancies, she feels too depressed and has little physical energy, to further her career.

Physical health may be another reason to commit suicide, especially terminal illnesses or severe physical handicaps. The suicidal may feel they are a burden on friends and relations. They may also feel that they cannot come to terms with the loss of a limb or the loss of an active lifestyle. The suicidal act may seem to relieve all pain and suffering for the suicidal and the family, as it seems to the suicidal to offer less pain.

Mental illness is a frequent cause of suicidal ideation, as with depression and schizophrenia. It may seem like a life sentence of suffering and despair, especially where the client lives alone and is unemployed. Suicide may seem to be a logical answer to an emotional state that offers no relief from unhappiness and mental torture. Medication may prove unsuccessful in dealing with symptoms that have deeper psychological causes. It is the counsellor's task to unlock the hidden motivations of a suicidal client and help a stronger adult ego to reason out a more positive alternative to the patient's suffering. However, reasoning capabilities may be impaired by the side effects of psychiatric drugs. The client need to wait until they have reduced their drugs.

The therapist must with empathy reach out to the client's individual process of thinking and reasoning, so that the patient feels there is someone who understands her and whom she can trust. Only then can psychotherapy assist with solving the causes of the client's suffering and help them cope with their suicidal feelings.

The DSM-IV considers thoughts and beliefs about death and dying. It is crucial for the therapist to understand how clients define death, as this may affect a client's will to live. An atheist may see suicide as bringing about an end to all suffering and personal frustration and sexual orientation difficulties e.g. a homosexual or lesbian client who is facing disapproval from her parents and from discrimination at work, where there is name calling and lack of promotion to senior positions.

Religious beliefs may affect the suicidal if the sufferer feels strongly that there is something better on the "other side" of death, e.g. a glorious heaven where there is no pain and one meets all their dead relatives and friends. However, certain religions may view suicide as a sin and the religious client may feel she will be sent to Hell if she takes her life

Alternatively, religious and political beliefs may encourage "altruistic" suicidal thinking, such as in the case of Hunger strikers or Buddhist monks setting fire to themselves. These mostly take place in extreme economic and political turmoil However, such "moralistic" types are the least likely to see therapists because of their strongly held religious convictions. E.g. a catholic may prefer to express their suffering to a priest in confession. Also, it may be argued that the strict moral and ethical rules of religious obedience, can create guilt and repression of natural desires. One example are sexual awakenings in Catholic Seminaries, leading to a feeling of a need to be punished and that punishment could be suicide So, suicidal ideation may increase as a result of feeling "sinful".. ..

To conclude the reasons for contemplating suicide are complex and the main factors seem to be the presence of forms of stress, hopelessness and helplessness. However, the main factor that is prominent is the presence of depression or other mental disorders. Having said that altruistic or political suicidal acts are other reasons why persons may take one's life.

In other words, the suicidal person wishes to put an end to unbearable emotional or physical pain. The suicidal individual has many thoughts about how, when and by what means they wish to commit suicide. This is often accompanied by anger, rage, grief, loneliness, despair, emptiness and low self esteem.

It should be said that insecurity about housing, money, the breakdown of relationships, bullying at work and school, inadequate parenting and the loss of love all create stress and depression. Any of these factors may encourage clients to contemplate suicide.

Q6.2/ Evaluate the factors which might increase a client's risk of suicide

I will answer by considering which factors are most likely to increase the risk of a client's suicide.

Counsellors need to be aware of those clients who are most at risk. I.e. those who have a history of mental disorders, psychiatric care and a previous history of suicidal attempts.Clients who are addicted to illegal drugs or alcohol are also at a greater risk of suicide, particularly those who feel less inhibited to attempt suicide due to the drug effects. It needs to be considered that alcohol and some drugs, like Heroin, also have a depressive effect on some users.

Depression can increase the need to commit suicide. This may also include clients aged 11 to 25 years and those over 50 years, who are most at risk. Young people may have high hopes of attainment and freedom that are unrealistic in this highly competitive, consumer-led society. Likewise, mature people may have married, divorced, had Children and a career and yet they feel they have underachieved and are "losers".Again, depression may set in and suicide may seem the only "way out".. Alternatively older people may have not achieved any of these aforementioned ideals and may feel that life is rather pointless..A lack of status or purpose may increase the risk of suicide.

The Mental Disorders

a/ Depression

Some 90% of suicidal attempts are by those who suffer from depression and are up to 100 times more likely to commit suicide than those who don't. suffer depression. The counsellor should not exclude those suffering from Bipolar disorder, Schizoaffective disorder (schizophrenia depression), eating disorders and personality disorders; especially BPD. The therapist should know that these disorders have traits of depression too, as they may be overlooked or misdiagnosed. It was long considered that schizophrenics, by definition, did not suffer from depression, so the sufferer was considered less likely than say, a manic-depressive (Bi-polar) to commit suicide. Any illness with a component of depression is likely to increase the risk of suicide.

Those who are at most risk with depression are those who have just been discharged from psychiatric care and decided to kill themselves as their illness improved..
This is usually after an upswing from a severe black or psychotic depression.

It may be argued that those who are most depressed lack the energy and initiative to carry out a suicide but these are the ones whom are more likely to eventually commit suicide. The most important time to assess the risk of suicide is when a patient is on an upswing from depression, as the client has the energy to carry out a suicidal act.

The counsellor should not assume that the suicidal risk has decreased, simply because the client acts "normal"."Socratic questioning, such as what are you thinking, feeling and uncomfortable body language may offer some clues to the client's intentions. The counsellor may notice contradictory verbal statements, such as "I'm going on holiday abroad" or " I am going to teach abroad". The client may appear miserable or sad, whilst making out of character remarks.Body language, such as folded arms, crossed legs or facial frowning may denote an underlying denial of suicidal feelings to the counsellor's questions. Patients in emotional denial are also at a greater risk of attempting suicide and this factor needs to be taken seriously by the therapist.

The British Holistic Medical Association suggests that between 50 and 75% of those who have clinical depression , are at high risk of suicide. This higher risk factor may be lessened by taking prescribed anti-depressant medication.However,any talk of suicide by a depressive should be taken seriously and assessed by a counsellor, no matter what the severity of suicidal risk is to the patient or level of psychiatric care that the client is receiving.

b/ Schizophrenia

Schizophrenics or schizo-affetcives are at high risk of suicide, especially those who have auditory hallucinations compelling them to kill themselves, as well as visual hallucinations that are extremely frightening.One could argue that schizophrenics suffer from some of the highest level of fear and anxiety, when compared to other disorders such as Bi-polar Disorder. Indeed, I argue that fear is a cause of many mental health conditions and a desire to end the fear may result in an increased risk of suicide.

They are most at risk if they are paranoid and have come off their antipsychotic medication, as well as receiving poor community care or isolation from family and society due to prejudice, such as schizophrenics considered as "dangerous", by the media e.g. a headline on a newspaper highlighting a murder by a "schizophrenic." This kind of tabloid reporting only serves to stigmatise schizophrenics and to isolate the client more from her community;there may be an increase in the risk of suicide from the isolation and stigma that schizophrenics have to bear.

Therapists must continually monitor the degree of care in the community and as to whether or not the client is regularly taking her medication. Communication with other health professionals, such as psychiatrists may be desirable to assess the level of care. A lack of care in the community may increase the risk of suicide.

c/ Border Personality Disorder

Clients with BPD are at greater risk when high levels of paranoia, relationship problems, aggression, impulsivity, self harm and emptiness or loneliness are present. There may be strong feelings of "pointlessness" or "badness", accompanied by guilt and feeling "dirty", especially where the client has been abused. There maybe a strong sense of a need to be punished for her "badness" and suicide may seem a logical answer and punishment.

Where impulsivity is present suicide may be acted upon very easily, especially when accompanied by self harm..

All client's suffering from personality disorders are at greater risk from suicide, where there maybe some other factors present, e.g. alcohol and drug addiction, substance abuse, lack of effective psychiatric medication or poor care. These factors need to be understood by counsellors because they indicate an increased risk of suicide, especially where depression is also present.

d/ <u>Eating Disorders</u>

Clients with anorexia nervosa are at an increased risk of committing suicide, as they are 40 times more likely than the general public to attempt suicide. Much of this maybe due to a great deal of self hatred because of concern about their weight. The counsellor needs to ask the client if they have accompanying depression, as this may increase the risk of suicide.

<u>MAJOR CONTRIBUTORY FACTORS TO THE RISK OF SUICIDE</u>

It is important that the therapist considers the following factors that may contribute towards to a risk of suicide. The counsellor needs to offer reassurance, empathy and appropriate interventions to the client, where these factors are prevalent.

a/ Physical Illness

The therapist needs to assess reduced mobility, lack of quality of life and terminal illnesses, e.g. cancer, may induce depression and thus increase the risk of suicide.

b/ Loss of reputation or status

Demotion or redundancy at work, especially in times of economic recession. The therapist needs to ask how this has impacted on his family and social life.

Failing to meet employers demands of conduct, e.g. a teacher who lacks the ability to exercise discipline and is sacked. The therapist needs to reassure the client of her abilities and self worth.Loss of self esteem due to a career that gave the client purpose may put the patient at an increased risk of suicide, since we all need a sense of purpose and belonging. A client who doesn't feel she belongs to a community may become suicidally depressed.

c/ Anxiety and stress

Clients with unbearable stress due to heavy work loads or postnatal depression due to increased responsibilities, poor results as a student and feelings of perfectionism, leading to unrealistic expectations may all trigger depression and the risk of suicide. The therapist must assess the effect stress is having on the client and offer coping techniques, e.g. relaxation and breathing exercises.

d/ Explosive Events

A sudden traumatic situation, such as the horrors of war, a row with a boy or girlfriend, a sudden death of a close relative or friend in an accident, may all increase suicidal risk. If the trauma is only temporary then short term psychotherapy is possible or if it is PTSD then analysis over a longer period, with perhaps prescribed medication from a GP or psychiatrist may be necessary

e/ Changes in Behaviour

Hoarding pain killers, psychiatric medication, weapons, e.g. sharp knives, ropes, shotguns etc, are more obvious signs of increased risk factors. The therapist needs to ask about the availability of the means to take one's life at the client's home and all sharp or hard, removable objects, must be removed from the counsellor's practice.

.

The client maybe visiting wild and remote areas over repeated times, where they are unlikely to be discovered. This is apparent when there is definite desire to end one's life and the client has sufficient willpower to override the powerful human will to live. Another factor that increases the risk of actual suicide is one where the client attempts to conceal their plans to die.. The client may also drop hints or gesture that they are tired of living. Any hints must be seriously examined by the therapist, as these clients are the most likely to succeed in committing suicide. Also, a tidy client may suddenly become untidy in appearance or lacking personal hygiene. It must be said that a usually untidy client may do the opposite and become meticulously dressed or obsessively clean in the home or make a premature will. Anything out of the ordinary life of a client should be noted by the therapist and relevant questions asked, to prevent suicide.

The risk factors that might increase a client's risk of suicide are complex but fear, stress, anxiety and traumatic changes in lifestyle, may cause mental illness and increase depression: the main factor in suicidal attempts..

Q6.3

<u>Discuss the possible processes to be followed if a client informed you they were suicidal</u>

The therapist firstly should ask fundamental, thought provoking, questions to assess the client's risk of suicide, on a continuum from low to high risk. Then consider the steps to be taken which are appropriate for a client in a low risk category and steps to be undertaken for those at high risk.

1/ <u>Does the client have a history of self harm or any suicidal tendencies?</u>

If not then the client is at a low risk but this does not always confer with young people or anyone facing an explosive event, e.g. a family row or bankruptcies. The latter may be at higher risk, even if there is no suicidal history. Young people may have no history of self harm or suicide, yet as teenagers they may begin to contemplate suicide. This especially holds true where there is a history of neglect, physical, emotional or sexual abuse.

Again, the counsellor may ask tentative questions concerning any history of childhood trauma.

An indirect way of revealing any abuse is to use guided imagery or fantasy work e.g. the client watches herself, in fantasy,, at a cinema, watching a movie of her own life and is asked to project emotions onto her own chosen animated characters e.g. people, animals, birds or objects.The animated features represent the hidden emotional state of the patient and this may reveal the unconscious desire to attempt suicide.

2/ Is the client depressed?

If yes, then the patient is at high risk but maybe the depression is mild and non-clinical, e.g. the blues, or a need of gain attention or even hurt others, e.g. families, friends, partners etc. If the depression is moderate then there may be no imitative to die but one needs to assess the energy levels to carry out a suicide.Any variant of depression must be taken seriously and other professionals should be informed e.g. a psychiatrist, social worker or a community nurse.

3/ Is there a plentiful supply of suicidal weapons or other means to commit suicide at home, college or work?

If a client, for example, is a farmer who tells me that he intends to kill himself and has access to a firearm; than he is at high risk. Alternatively, if a client says they are going to hang themselves then if a rope, wire, flex etc, and these means are not readily available, then the client is at low risk. One should always check to see if the client has prescribed medication, as suicide by overdose if is one of the most common means of suicide. If so, a CPN or psychiatrist may limit the dosage by the use of weekly Dosettes. Of course, the client may supplement their intake of poisons by buying painkillers, such as paracetamol, over the counter at pharmacies.

.

4/ Do you want to die?

If the answer to this direct question is yes, then obviously the client may be at high risk, but replying yes maybe an attempt to call for help from the therapist.and to call attention to an immediate stressful situation, e.g. a family break up.If yes, the client may not be in immediate danger but requesting relief and help from unbearable stress. Any "yes" answer has to be taken seriously and acted upon. The counsellor may need to break client confidentiality and contact the client's social worker, community nurse or psychiatrist. The psychotherapist may also direct the client to report to the local casualty department, where her needs will be assessed.

Admission to a psychiatric unit may be necessary.The direct question maybe too uncomfortable and may not offer up the correct state of the patient. Asking more subtle questions may prove more useful, such as asking the client about her feelings, mood and what is uppermost in her mind. How depressed or stressed the client is, may be elicited through questions that ask the patient as to what, if any, plans she has for the evening or weekend. If the patient replies she is going out with friends to the cinema or any other social event involving close friends this may suggest that the client is in a good or positive mood. Insofar as the "friends" are not the stressor and the cause of the client's distress.

Sensitive and indirect questioning is arguably less stressful for the client, than asking if the client wants to die, and hopefully won't add to the patient's already stressful situation.

If "no", the patient may be at low risk, except to hide her real intention to die, from a decision that the client has already made to kill herself. However, the client may not wish to distress the therapist and cause the intervention of her family, friends and doctors and prevent her from carrying out suicide. Most suicide attempts are a cry for help but all should be taken seriously. .A "yes" answer doesn't always mean a real need to die and likewise a "No" answer may conceal a real desire to die.

The counsellor needs to take notes of the client's mood, feelings and thoughts and any body language, such as a withdrawn, head down posture and little eye contact Anything out of the ordinary: behaviour and speech should be noted, as this may suggest depression and a higher risk of suicide.

5/ What has stopped you from committing suicide in the past?

If there are strong preventive or deterrent factors present, then the client maybe at low risk, e.g. loving, caring support,. a partner, a concerned parent or a helpline, such as the Samaritans. If there are no deterrents then the client is at high risk, except maybe if the patient is on psychiatric medication that help alleviate the symptoms.

Also, as the eminent Psychologist, Dorothy Rowe, argued the client may resist suicide if they believe that by taking one's life they leave a legacy of suicide with friends or family i.e. children or adults may imitate the suicidal when they face stress or depression, particularly when they reach the client's age.Alternatively, the young may consider the suicide of someone close as pointless, lacking courage or even "bad".However, the deceased suicide victim may lessen the courage of of others, when they face similar difficulties in life.

A warm, caring and empathetic counsellor is in a strong position to influence the suicidal. Some even allow their clients to call them in an emergency like suicide. Again, the counsellor's professional body may discourage the "good samaritan" counsellor, as it may encourage a precedence and create dependency. I feel that the counsellor has a moral and ethical duty to prevent suicide at all cost and some do, despite the obvious intrusion on the therapist's time and the added stress.

Suicidal clients whom have strong religious beliefs may be evade suicide by prayer and contemplation. Non-believers and a few cults that don't believe in a saviour may view worship as ineffective and life as pointless. However, some religious cults and more orthodox religions offer an ideal heaven that is a place where we all fulfill our human desires that can not be realised on Earth. The promise of a utopia beyond the grave may be more attractive than the troubles on our planet and this may encourage believers to take their lives. This may not apply where suicide is seen as a sin or a "bad karma", where the believer may have to overcome his suicidal tendencies, when he is reborn.

Finally, suicide may be prevented by admission to hospital, especially where there exists an observation room. Very little can stop a suicidal client if they are absolutely determined to kill themselves but one has to override the powerful will to live and as far as hope persists suicide can be stopped.

6/ Do you have any positive future plans?

If yes, then the will to live is stronger than the will to die and it would be difficult for the patient to override the "life urges" with "destructive urges". Where there is hope that life will get better and there is a will to take positive action, the patient may have positive plans. The plans may be small, perhaps to see a counsellor or psychiatrist but it is a sign that there is some hope that with help, life will improve.. Other basic plans, such as deciding to do some spring cleaning or painting the walls, suggest there is a will to simply live.

The counsellor needs to be aware that a need to be unusually tidy, may suggest that the client is preparing for suicide. More positive plans maybe joining a self help group e.g. anger or anxiety management groups. Others may include going to a pub restaurant with friends, joining a dating site, getting married, moving to a more desirable home, having children, going on holiday, studying a creative course that helps fulfill the client's potential,changing a job or career to a less stressful occupation and learning to drive and buying a new car. The list is endless but all the aforementioned strongly suggest a great deal of hope and will. It is self evident that a strong capacity to plan a better life suggests no will to commit suicide.

If the patient has no future plans, this may suggest a temporary bout of depression or the client without any hope maybe considering suicide. However, the will to get out of bed in the morning, wash and brush teeth and then see her counsellor implies some will power- to go on living. A simple plan to see her therapist suggests a positive plan to get better. The psychotherapist needs to harness this glimmer of hope and will to live. The counsellor may gently suggest the client sees her GP and possibly the doctor may offer prescribed anti-depressants or refer her to a psychiatrist. A CPN may help with accompanying the patient on trips to parks, shopping centres or the cinema.

The psychotherapist may help in sessions by asking the client, if she has felt depressed before, when and what was happening at those times. For example, the client may remember being sad and lonely at school or home and suffering emotional cruelty by her father or teacher(s). The client may feel "responsible" for any abuse or neglect and the counsellor may help reframe the incident(s). The counsellor may ask the client to describe the incidents in detail e.g. sights, sounds, smells, colours, speech or any physical abuse. This may result in a cathartic release of fear, anger or grief, that can be safely released in the sessions.

It is very important that any cathartic work is done with a qualified therapist and never on one's own. There is a danger in the cathartic work being an end in itself and not a means to find greater emotional freedom. Also, a client who has no plans and is in deep depression must be asked if she is happy to continue with the reframing exercises. The client may not be ready for some time, even after years of therapy.

A suicidal client lacks reasoning and a strong adult ego state; a counsellor may strengthen the rational thinking of the client by exploring positive alternatives to suicide, e.g. developing creativity. The suicidal ideation may be reduced by the counsellor offering empathy and non-judgemental listening. The counsellor should avoid patronising by moralising about the rights and wrongs of feeling suicidal. It should never be seen as a weak or cowardly outcome, as this will cause a distance between a client and therapist and reduce the trust the patient has in the counsellor's techniques.

.

If the client has no future, positive plans and is depressed and suicidal, then the counsellor may , with great empathy, ask the patient to describe with much detail as possible, how the client plans to commit suicide. This may provide a release from the powerful desires to kill themselves and produce alternative practical solutions to seemingly irresolvable stress or unhappiness, I.e. to provide the client with a vision of a "life worth living" and offer hope and good reasons to live, e.g. suggest to the client that, she may be a strong adult role model as a survivor and give courage to children and young people. Never dare the suicidal patient to commit suicide , as they may just do it in a depressed state.

Processes to be followed if the client is at high risk of suicide.

If any doubt as to what is to be done the counsellor must contact NHS direct for invaluable assistance and assessment of the patient's condition. If the mental health laws prescribe it, the suicidal client may be sectioned or admitted to a in care psychiatric unit. If there are injuries that are not life threatening then a nurse at a local GP's surgery may deal with cuts or wounds on the client's body.

A follow up appointment with a GP or psychiatrist may be needed. The client's confidentiality will need to be broken, as agreed in the client-counsellor agreement at the start of sessions.

A local pharmacist can recommend first aid for minor injuries, e.g. bandages, lotions for burns etc.

A counsellor should not be sworn to secrecy. It is often traumatic coping with suicidal clients. Therapists may need to speak to colleagues, a supervisor or a crisis intervention helpline for extra support. The therapist must understand their own limitations and seek more objective advice from other suitably qualified, professionals i.e. a supervisor, other counsellors, the client's GP, psychiatric nurse, social worker or a psychiatrist..

To conclude, talking therapies are beneficial for suicidal clients who are at low risk and feel hopeless. All clients should be helped to see the positive aspects of their lives, which may go unnoticed when a client feels suicidal. By seeing the positive things in their lives the suicidal can find hope and see that solutions to their distress is possible. A very good method for counselling clients who feel hopeless, is to ask the client to reflect on past experiences, hobbies, and activities she once enjoyed and ask her if she would enjoy doing them again in the future.

The psychotherapist can help by asking the patient to visualise in detail in an imaginary movie, all the major friends or family enjoying themselves. The client may enter the imaginary movie on a large screen and play her own part. This reminds the client that she did have happier times and it is possible to collaborate with the counsellor to create a plan based on those enjoyable activities.

If the patient is hopeless, then the therapist may deter a suicidal act by pointing out that suicide can be painful, messy act that can, if it fails, bring about long term physical harm.. However, if hopelessness turns to actual threats , that are well planned and imminent, then referrals to other mental health or psychiatric services are vital and maybe life saving. All talk of suicide must be taken seriously, even if the threat to life is seen as a low or high risk.

Q6.7 Evaluate the available techniques and tools when helping someone stop harming.

Self harm is a coping measure for a client who self harms, whom has deep psychological distress, that the client cannot put into words or even thoughts easily. It is often accompanied by loneliness and often that is the time, when the self injurious is most at risk. Self harm is frequently.an attempt to discharge powerful destructive urges, such as anger, fear, rage and even suicidal feelings by inflicting harm on the self harmer's' body i.e. arms, wrists and legs etc. Self harm roughly affetcs 1% of the population and It is most common in young, female adults and adolescents. Self harm maybe an effect of bullying, abuse and neglect at home or at school. Sexual abuse and rape are major causes of self harm.

The therapist needs to respect the need for a client to self harm, as it offers temporary relief from intense anguish. The psychotherapist must never try to force the self injurious to stop harming herself, as self harm is often the only way the client can prevent suicide. If the client has inflicted serious, life threatening injuries, then phone for emergency help.

The therapist needs to wait for the client to gain trust in him and be calm enough to be responsive to counselling. It is vital that the therapist has permission from the client to explore the underlying hurt beneath the self harm, or the client may terminate the sessions too early. Also, the counsellor must not respond in shock or disgust at what the self harming client says or does. The reason being is the client may feel ashamed or guilty that she has caused the therapist to be upset.

The counsellor may diffuse much of the fear and anger, that may accompany self harm, by asking the client when she first felt like self harming. Questions that the psychotherapist may ask the patient are: describe in detail the context of the first memory of feeling depressed? Also, what occurred in detail; the people involved; what they said and did, the colours, clothing worn, unusual smells, shapes and bodily sensation. Was anyone informed of the initial trauma and did they take any action? The aim of this dialogue is to discharge any repressed negative emotions e.g. fear, anger, grief etc. These are the most important emotions behind self harm. The client's answers may reveal that she feels "guilty"or responsible for the initial trauma.

The counsellor by encouraging the client to talk candidly about her traumas or abuse, allows the client to reframe who the real guilty parties were and that the client has no need to feel guilty or ashamed, about what she experienced. It should be emphasized that any talk about abuse, trauma and harm may be extremely unsettling for the client to convey memories or negatively felt emotions.

The psychotherapist may need to gain great confidence, by the client, in the counsellor's methods before any exploration of the past traumas can be explored in sessions i.e. the counsellor may ask about the client's present difficulties and events..

Self harming carries the threat of disability or death but it is important to see that most who self harm do not wish to cause serious harm to themselves. Indeed it is a really a call for help and to cope with destructive feelings, that if are not channelled into self harm could cause suicide. If the self harm becomes a serious threat to the client's life or causes serious injuries-request that the client attends casualty or emergency treatment at her local NHS surgery.

Self harm is manifested in many forms, such as scalding, burning, cutting, slashing, poisoning, pulling hair, banging one's head, biting, overdosing on painkillers, falling from walls and buildings, etc. The list is extensive.

.

THERAPEUTIC TECHNIQUES AND TOOLS

There are many practical alternatives to self harming and the counsellor should be aware of the individual's needs, as patently what works for one may not help another. The counsellor's main consideration should be to offer the patient an alternative that is less harmful but hurts slightly; enough to stop the urge to self harm.
This will be dependant on the client's individual need to self harm; the greater the need to self mutilate the more powerful the tool.

The counsellor needs to be sensitive to those tools and techniques that reduce or prevent self harm, given that every client's needs are very personal. I.e. no one who self harms really wants to hurt themselves or even know why they self harm. However, self harming allows temporary relief from unbearable emotional pain and helps reduce the risk of the client killing themselves.

Some techniques may be calming and relaxing, like a hot bath, or possibly one of keeping active and busy, e.g. digging the garden. Breathing and meditation exercises, watching a favourite comedy movie or listening to a relaxing CD may help with prevention. Going for a walk in the country or in a park may help the client to feel "grounded", perhaps by hugging a tree. The counsellor should recommend the patient keeps a diary and adds to it daily, noting any patterns of thoughts, feelings and behaviour before or just following self harm.

The therapist can explore why the patient felt a certain way and what failed to or prevented the patient from self harming, based on the client's diary. The counsellor should recommend that the client carries a mobile phone with her, in order to talk to a close friend or an emergency or crisis line volunteer; when in distress.
A "safe box" containing objects that help prevent self harm may be recommended by the counsellor; these may include a rubber band that can be snapped against the wrist, some old newspaper to tear violently or to hit a hard surface with, a red felt pen to colour the areas of the body which the patient usually harms, a favourite CD to play loudly, a comedy DVD like Airplane, or self help book and perhaps a shell from a happy holiday by the sea to remind her of pleasant and more positive times.

It would be a good idea to keep the daily diary in the "safe box" too, as the client can then write down any success with the preventative measures. The more calming techniques, like a walk in a park or a hot bath, may prove useful for those who self harm and have intense anxiety and restlessness. Whereas, aggressive cathartic methods like beating pillows or screaming to loud music may be suitable for client's with intense grief or rage. Arguably, a safe box is only safe when hidden away from other members of the family or abusive partners who don't understand and are critical of the self harming. This only adds to the suffering and loneliness that the client maybe feeling. Indeed, the support and empathy of friends, partners or family members is invaluable for the client's recovery and well being. Indeed, a sympathetic partner or parent may suggest counselling to the client before the client causes severe harm to herself.

If the urge to self mutilate is overwhelming then some alternative pain or force should be suggested by the counsellor, e.g. screaming to loud music, bashing pillows and throwing them hard against the wall or lying on a mattress and lashing it with both arms and legs; whilst screaming and swearing. Rubbing ice cubes vigorously on the skin or whacking a ruler on the palm of the hand may also add to the prevention of serious bodily harm.

To summarise,

When dealing with a patient who self harms the counsellor should avoid laying down firm rules about the right way to prevent self harming and be flexible about the tools and techniques to be undertaken by the patient. The therapist must understand that self harm is a coping device for powerful emotional distress and no one wants to hurt themselves.

Self harm maybe the only way the client can cope with painful emotions and may seem to the patient as the only option open to them.

Not all relevant techniques and tools to alleviate self harm have been discussed here and arguably some like sucking lemons may have little if any use at all. Other techniques using hard objetcs, such as rulers may actually stimulate harsh memories and flashbacks of abuse in childhood.Thus increasing the intolerable emotional pain in the client.It could be argued that techniques, like cathartic screaming, may cause dependency on "bizzare" behaviour and medication may prove more effetcive e.g. tranquilisers. However, some medications cause dependency and don't get at the underlying psychodynamics of traumas and self harm.

Therefore, all possible tools and techniques should be discussed between the client and the therapist; not ruling out any self harm if the client sees it as the only option to avoid suicide or life threatening injuries. The self harming client needs to be in charge of the safe alternative techniques and tools they use, if restimulation and harrowing flashbacks are to be avoided and the client is to remain safe and stable.

================================

ASSIGNMENT 7.1

_____

Q.1/ <u>Abuse and trauma could be seen as a cause for most mental health conditions. True or False? Explain your answer.</u>

Before answering the question of whether or not abuse and trauma causes most mental health conditions - I wish to define trauma and abuse, then consider the main types of abuse and trauma, that may cause mental ill health. Then, I will attempt to explain the likely illnesses that may arise from each major type of abuse or trauma. Finally, I will consider as to whether or not most mental health conditions are caused by abuse or trauma: True or False?

The term abuse comes from the Latin meaning "misused" and so one can see how easily it can be applied to maltreatment or assaults, improper use of power or position, corrupt practice and disclosures, i'll purpose, and verbal insults. As well as manipulation of another.

Trauma originates from the Greek word meaning, "wound".So, misuse of another can cause a physical or psychological wound or injury. A disturbing experience may lead to shock, stress and confusion. So, what are the major types of abuse or trauma, misuse or wound, that can lead to mental illness? And specifically, what mental health conditions are likely to arise.

There are many varied types of abuse and traumas that may occur throughout many cultures and social environments.

There are four basic types of abuse that I intend to focus on: Physical, emotional, sexual and one of neglect. All of which can cause stress, shock and trauma.

Physical abuse is the striking of someone with a hard hand or object., arguably against the will of another. Physical abuse also may include trapping someone in a small confined space, such as a room without windows. Also, it extends to gagging, tying up, burning or sleep deprivation. Confinement in a small space, especially without windows, may cause nightmares, insomnia and lead to claustrophobia: a fear of confined spaces.

Physical abuse may include hitting with a fist, a cane, a paddle, throwing a child against a wall or onto the floor. Some physical abuse occurs when the State uses its powers against dissenters or protesters, such as in the miners' strike of 1983, or more recently in the coup in Turkey during 2016. Physical abuse includes domestic attacks and neglect, as in the case of wife or spouse beatings and the lack of appropriate care and welfare of the families children. These examples usually involve the police or social workers and culprits may be charged and compelled to face justice in a court of law. Abused children may be taken into care, such as foster homes and vulnerable female victims may be offered protective women's shelters..This may lead to depression and anxiety, long after the abuse has ceased. Flashbacks and fear of being attacked or raped may cause PTSD and social phobia.The abused client may also become suicidal, as they may feel trapped.

It is important to note that not all victims will suffer poor mental health, indeed some will speedily recover and return to their usual way of life. Whilst other "victims" may continue to experience ill health for many months or years. Also not all abuse occurs in the home environment, it may manifest itself in schools, workplaces and even in the streets e.g. bullying, harassment, sectarian and racial attacks.All claims of physical abuse must be taken seriously by the therapist..It is important to realise that abuse, like bullying, of a child may have serious mental health consequences that continue into adulthood e.g.assaults on children by members of families or teaching staff can render the child extremely withdrawn, depressed, anxious, lacking confidence and possibly suicidal.

Early intervention by compassionate professionals to prevent on-going cruelty, such as counselling or law enforcement, can help the juvenile recover more rapidly and avoid the prolonged agony of mental ill health. Arguably, some gentle corporal punishment in schools or homes with the use of the hand may be justified as good discipline, prevention of delinquency and less harmful emotionally, compared to continual criticism and nagging..

Sexual abuse is the unlawful and inappropriate sexual contact between an adult or a child, usually a member of the same family, or another authoritative figure or older teenager. It has to be said that a child is unable physically, emotionally or intellectually able to protect themselves from abuse, So, the law is there to protect the innocents.

Sexual abuse ranges from verbal suggestions, fondling, kissing to attempted or actual intercourse. The figures show that girls are more likely to be abused than boys, 38% of girls and 16% of boys before they reach adulthood.

The abuser often manipulates the child victim by suggesting sexual activity as a child's game and will blame the abused for the acts, which may confuse and cause guilty feelings in the child. Thus the child victim may see the abuse as their own fault and the abuser as innocent.

Feelings of low self esteem, confusion, guilt, "dirtiness", depression, anxiety, panic attacks, eating disorders, borderline personality disorder,self harm, self hate and suicidal attempts may follow from abuse. The abused victim may have serious difficulty in trusting other adults, as a grown adult, and may fear sexual intercourse with another of his own age. However, other victims may become sexually promiscuous and there maybe little or no fear of sexual intercourse. Arguably most sexual predators have been sexually abused themselves at an early age and the abuser is, in most incidents, known to the victim.

The therapist needs to reassure the victim of abuse that their symptoms and emotions are an appropriate reaction to abuse. Then, the counsellor should help the client to re-evaluate her feelings of guilt and learn to see the perpetrator of abuse as the guilty wrongdoer.

Verbal or emotional abuse, such as "nagging", endless criticism, belittling, name calling and spoken threats, can be just as harmful as physical abuse except it carries no bodily injuries. It can therefore be difficult to prove, especially if there are no witnesses.

Verbal abuse or bullying can take place in schools, workplaces or at home. Verbal bullying can lead to social withdrawal, depression, schizophrenia, mania, social anxiety or phobias, isolation, and even suicide. The counsellor may refer the depressed and suicidal to their GP or to a psychiatrist for relevant medication. Social phobias and anxiety may be helped by joining a self help group organised by sufferers of these illnesses.

Other forms of abuse include domestic violence, elderly neglect and workplace bullying.

Domestic violence is the abuse of another whom is deemed as vulnerable, this includes the abuse of a spouse, or a homosexual partner. The abuser of his wife may also abuse his children; and aggressive men who attack children are more likely to be cruel to pets, where there exists a psychotic element in the aggressor.. Some psychotic abuse may result from misuse and overuse of cannabis and other illegal drugs, rendering the assailant paranoid and even schizophrenic. Abused men are far less likely to confess to being abused by a woman because of shame and to avoid being seen as "weak". The trust and love that the abused felt for their partner may be broken and feelings of being violated and guilty may present themselves. The therapist's role is to allow the victim to talk freely about their unpleasant experiences and build up trust in adult figures; firstly- the therapist

The male victim may become withdrawn, unusually quiet, non-assertive and possibly masochistic: allowing females to take advantage of himself. Arguably, no major mental illness results from the abusive woman..

Elderly neglect may range from hitting or slapping to withholding their food and medication or over-sedation. In a few cases medication may be unduly increased to dangerous levels, where the mature adult's behaviour is over controlled and the toxicity may lead to a premature death. The elderly may be isolated from friends and relations by their "carers" and this compounds their already loss of life-long friends and partners.Such isolation and distress may provoke a depressive response and the patient's will to live.Suicidal behaviour may include refusing food, liquids and drugs and even removal of any saline or food tubes from the body.

.

The therapist should report any elderly abuse to the nursing home's management, the social services or the police in cases of physical cruelty or theft of money and possessions.

Workplace bullying is also prevalent and is carried out by men and women, including acts by managers and supervisors. It may include withholding paper or computer data and discs.; as well as talking detrimentally about a colleague in listening distance or spreading malicious gossip to their supervisors. There may be actual inappropriate touch and invasion of space, as well as endangering the victim by setting up dangerous situations, e.g. being g told to wait on the top of a ladder for a long period without help. Where the victim is hard working and conscientious, such as a high achieving teacher who is popular with his students, his colleagues may become overly envious and conspire to remove him.

The client's colleagues maybe mentally demented and seek to destroy the client's career because of their own inadequacy. This may cause depression, anxiety and suicidal ideation.

In severe cases, the client may have a nervous breakdown, resulting in hospital admission and a major mental disorder e.g. Bipolar Disorder or schizophrenia. The therapist may suggest that the abused talk to their GP or psychiatrist, with a view of taking sickness leave and undertaking less stressful voluntary work.

It is true to say that forms of bullying, abuse or trauma do often lead to mental illnesses such as anxiety, depression, PTSD, Borderline Personality Disorders, phobias and in extreme cases schizophrenia and suicide. But, individuals cope with traumas differently and some overcome them without any need of therapy or medication.Others spend a lifetime in psychiatric care with severe mental disorders, such as schizophrenia or PTSD, going in and out of Primary care in mental health units. Also, some may recover from abuse or trauma quickly and pass it off as a hurdle in life to overcome.

Also, there are many other factors that may cause mental disorders, such as genetic or socio-economic influences. Genetic inherited characteristics, poverty and the presence or absence of loving, hugging and firm but fair parenting - contribute to how one responds to trauma and abuse and whether or not an individual develops mental ill health.

Abuse and trauma may cause most mental illnesses but there is no evidence that determines that all victims will respond to abuse and trauma in the same way. We are all different psychologically and physiologically.

Nature, our inherited features, and nurture, our socio-economic status or class with warm, loving and protective parenting; all help shape how we respond to abuse and trauma and whether one will develop mental ill health. The more vulnerable the child or adult, then the more likely traumas or abuse will cause a mental disorder.

Q7.2

<u>Your client discloses they are currently being abused and are considered vulnerable. What do you do?</u>

The counsellor must assess the risk to the abused child or vulnerable adult and the need to act swiftly if the abused is in imminent or life threatening danger. This would apply to most forms of abuse, especially physical or sexual abuse.If this is so, then the therapist has a legal duty to override client confidentiality and report the abuse to the police, social services or their governing supervisory body. The counsellor should seek disclosure of information from their patient, if this is not practical then the social or psychiatric services should be notified. The psychiatric team may, under law, section the client if she is at imminent danger to herself, by her husband, a family member, someone intimately known to her- tutor or preacher- or a member of the public..

If the risk assessment determines that the client is at low risk, then the counsellor should allow the patient to speak freely about the abuse at a pace and means of their own choosing e.g. via telephone. The therapist's questions must be open-ended and totally free of expectations or judgements concerning alleged abuse.

Although, all declarations of abuse should be taken seriously, it must be borne in mind that some accusations of abuse are false. It is not the position of the therapist to act as a legal judge but to help heal the mental wounds, wherever they arise and for whatever reasons.

This is the most challenging aspect of abuse counselling, as it often provokes strong emotions and opinions in the counsellor. Psychotherapy helps the patient overcome feelings of self-blame and guilt for "allowing" it to happen. Abuse is an unwanted mental or physical attack in all cases.

The counsellor can help the patient think more logically, in the adult ego state, and see themselves as not at fault and view their abuse as abnormal; reducing the need to disassociate their present feelings from the past abusive events. This may allow powerful emotions to surface, which the therapist can help the client to safe fully discharge e.g.grief by crying..

Where the abuse is ongoing the therapist needs to promote self confidence in the client, so that the abused may seek assistance from a close friend, a trusted teacher or an understanding parent. Help lines, like Childline or the Samaritans may be suggested or a shelter for the vulnerable, e.g. a ladies shelter whom have been subjected to domestic violence or emotional cruelty.

The following points of help for victims should be encouraged by therapists-
1/ Keep safe and have an escape plan for times of imminent danger
2/ Keep a mobile phone or money for a call box at hand
3/ Keep a diary of abuse; when it happened, where, what took place and outcomes that can be discussed in counselling sessions.

4/ Keep evidence of abuse, such as emails, photos, letters, recordings etc.

5/ Confide in a trusted neighbour, relation, friend, priest who may intervene.

6/ Tell the police and call "999" in an emergency or a crisis helpline , e.g. Childline or the National Domestic Violence Helpline etc.

7/ Go to a safe place in a house or school where there is a means of escape.

The confidentiality of the client may be overridden by the therapist, " where there is a clear risk of significant harm to the child…or serious harm to adults".

If the therapist feels that the client's needs cannot be served by him, then a referral to another counsellor or psychiatrist should be considered.

To conclude, it is imperative that the therapist acts speedily and professionally in the case of a client whom is currently being abused and is in a vulnerable group, such as a child; young person; or an elderly individual. The psychotherapist needs to give immediate comfort and empathy to the client, if possible establish who the alleged abuser is and where the abuse is taking place e.g. at home or college. Then call the police, the client's social worker, psychiatric unit or doctor. In life threatening or physical wound situations, the patient needs to be taken to an emergency or casualty unit. In cases of minor injuries, a nurse at a local GP's surgery may be able to clean and administer dressings to the client's wounds. Only after the aforementioned urgent procedures have been undertaken, can the psychotherapist begin to unlock the emotional wounds and work together, with the client, to heal them.

Q7.3

<u>Your client discloses they physically abused their child.</u>
<u>What would you do?</u>

Firstly, I would need to establish what my patient means by physical abuse and the severity of the "abuse."

If the abuse is one of simply disciplining their child by, for example, by a slap on the wrist or on the buttocks, after a verbal warning; this may not necessarily be of great concern. Corporal punishment in the home is currently legal in the UK, therefore it is arguably not a case for the police or social services. However, smacking is a violent act and may encourage violent behavior in the child in adolescence and adulthood, such as bullying or criminal acts, such as wife beating. I would argue that if the client discloses the physical abuse is over a long period and causes actual physical harm, e.g. a broken limb or bodily rupture caused by an assault, then immediate action is necessary i.e. contact the police or social services.

An important role of a counsellor is to keep confidentiality, be impartial and to be non-judgemental, this is tested to the limits by revelations of abuse. Personal opinions and assumptions must be kept out of the equation, if the counselling is to be balanced and effective. However, the counsellor cannot always maintain confidentiality if there is immediate risk of damage to the client, their child, another person or property. The patient must be informed, from the start, that confidentiality may be broken where the law requires it.

The relevant authorities must be told if the law requires it. " Where there is a significant risk of harm to a child".

The patient must clearly understand the laws governing confidentiality and the need to involve the Police, Social Services and other health carers. Once the client understands the legal requirements, then as a matter of care I would discuss the case with my supervisor and consult the moral and ethical guidelines of my professional governing body, then inform the Police, social workers, and other carers.

Once the client understands the legal requirements I would listen to the patient without judgement or prejudice. It is vital that the therapist doesn't reach any conclusions before hearing the client's whole story and keep personal feelings totally out of the counselling. The therapist should use open questioning and avoid presuming any conclusions. Listening to everything the client says, without presumptions, is vital if the counsellor is to fully understand the severity of abuse. The client may be confused as to whether a minor action, such as play fighting leads to a child crying, is a form of abuse. Also, the abuse may be more serious than the patient claims.

The parent client may feel guilty and admitting this is the first step to recovery. The counsellor must not verbally, or by body language, show disapproval of the patient's actions, as the client may feel great remorse or guilt and feel a need to punish themselves by attempted suicide. A no-suicide contract may help,especially if it is in writing and signed by the client. It is not binding but does carry some moral duty on the part of the patient..

The counsellor should keep accurate records or notes on what is said and what occurs in the sessions. The therapist must keep records of advice, suggestions, use of techniques and methods etc.

These records are invaluable for referring to the therapist's supervisor or to an authoritative body if the law requires it. If the therapist feels she feels incapable of counselling an abusive client, then the case should be referred to her supervisor or governing body.

Abuse raises very strong feelings and attitudes which a therapist may find stressful to cope with. So, It is important that the counsellor seeks support from her supervisor or other assisting organisation, e.g. the NSPCC . The welfare of the therapist, client and abused are of concern here but the therapist should act within the rules of a supervisory body, e.g. the BACP, and the law of the therapist's jurisdiction..

To conclude, the counsellor must act immediately if the child has been actually harmed and if the client has broken the law. The police and social services must be contacted where an abused child is in danger.The counselling of the adult should be non-judgemental and without any assumptions. Counselling should only follow clarification of the type of abuse and its severity, and only after relevant child protection teams have been informed of actual physical harm to the client's child.

Q4/ <u>Why could intimate relations be difficult for a client who has been sexually abused?</u>

Sexual abuse is an abuse of trust, affection and innocence, as well as an attack on a person's sexuality. i.e. sexual abuse can distort, limit and change the sexual orientation or desires of the abused. In some victims it can deter them from having any intimate relationships, reduce the nature and enjoyment of intimacy and in some victims it can transform their sexual identity e.g. a child who is abused may experience early homosexuality or promiscuity with older adults. However, homosexuality may be an innate, a genuine choice of sexual attraction or even a severe lack of nurturing and intimacy with either parent, both or none, as in the case of illegitimate children.

The attack on a child's trust and faith in adults is also an attack on the child's innate - intuition and wisdom; their own sense of what is right and wrong, which is cancelled out by the adult abuser. In effect, the child learns to trust the abusers own opinions and actions, whilst denying his own. In many cases the child may be "groomed" by an adult known to the young person, over a lengthy period and manipulate an innocent young person into sexual acts by the abuser acting as a child e.g. over the Internet.

The therapist's role here is to build up the trust in the abused child's own inner knowing and to learn to dismiss the abusers attitudes and opinions e.g. the paedophile may see his abusive actions as "normal" and healthy.

As a result of sexual abuse many survivors find their sexual attitudes and responses are affected e.g. an adult survivor may react angrily to any touch or talk of sex by another adult.. These effects may not be permanent but seriously hamper the enjoyment and pleasure of one's sexual activity with a partner..

Some abused clients will deny themselves any sexual contact or exploration and will often enter a phase of celibacy, to avoid being vulnerable and losing control over their own bodies. Others may become sexually promiscuous in an attempt to regain power over themselves, often by having the power to dismiss sex partners easily. This may be seen as a normal reaction to abuse and part of the healing process. It may only be temporary.

The effects of sexual abuse may present themselves immediately after the abusive acts or much later in life, e.g. after watching a programme on rape or abuse. The sexual dysfunction may not occur until one enters a loving and trusting relationship, where the abused may not be able to respond to genuine love and affection..

Here are some of the most common effects of sexual abuse-
1/ Avoiding or being scared of sex and being afraid of adult intercourse.
2/ Feeling obliged to have sex, especially when afraid of adults.
3/ Feeling disgust, anger or fear when tactile.
4/ Difficulties in becoming sexually aroused or reaching an orgasm.
5/ Experiencing flashbacks or nightmares, during or after sexual contact.
6/ Involving oneself in sadomasochistic sexual acts, involving violence or bondage..

7/ Difficulties in keeping to one partner for a long period or abruptly ending the affair.

8/ Having erection problems or vaginal pains.

9./ Low self esteem and having little self confidence e.g.in finding an enduring affair.

.

The counsellor should discover which of the above symptoms apply to her client, as not all of these may necessarily apply to one patient.

The abused client usually has a set of false beliefs of sex, such as abstention from sex or sex with children as acceptable. So, sexual acts in adulthood may be confused with sexual abuse in earlier life. Though sexual acts did take place, they were abnormal because they were not agreed to and the adult abuser used his power over the abused's body. So, the abused client may have difficulties with a relationship that doesn't involve domination by one partner over another..

It is important that the counsellor questions the client's false beliefs about appropriate consensual sex as the victim may be confused about what is appropriate and what is not acceptable. This may vary from one country to another, possibly due to social culture, religion, morality and laws.

The therapist must help the abused patient towards a safe, healthy and trusting sexual relationship with another adult; one that is uncomplicated by any sexual desire to assault children. It is vital that the abused client is not treated as a would be abuser, simply because they may have only known sex with abusive adults. This would almost certainly stigmatise the client and lead to mistrust and feelings of being misunderstood by the therapist. The client may not feel safe and terminate any future sessions.

The abused victim must be trusted and feel safe to talk freely and in detail about their past traumas, without any judgements or prejudice from the counsellor. To overcome any difficulty the client may have with intimacy, trust and safety must be established to encourage detailed, cathartic talking, as a means of dispersing the traumatic wounds.

Here is a set of well defined boundaries that can help the client feel safe with sex-

1/ It is okay to say no to any form of sexual activity at anytime.

2/ It is okay to ask for what one wants out of sex without shame or guilt.

3/ It is okay to say what one is feeling about different sexual acts.

4/ What is done in sex is private and no one's business, unless one agrees to sharing experiences.

5/ One is responsible for one's own sexual preferences and orgasms.

6/ Sexual thoughts and fantasies belong to oneself and need not be shared.

7/ One doesn't have to share details of previous sexual experiences or partners unless if health and safety is of concern.

8/ Both partners agree to be faithful sexually, unless if it is agreed that sexual relationships outside the partnership are acceptable..

9/ Both sexual partners agree to help each other with any consequences of sexual behaviour, e.g. re-stimulation of bodily or psychological hurt, or feelings of confusion and of guilt from past abuse.

Despite the above boundaries in intimate relationships - there may occur negative emotions during sexual acts: flashbacks, sickness, panic, pain, fear, confusion, sadness, tearfulness etc. These emotional responses are understandable reactions to the abused client's past traumas, and all sexual activity should be stopped, allowing time for some reflection on what triggered the emotion e.g.distinctive smells. The patient may be encouraged by the therapist to practice relaxation that enables the abused to switch attention to a happier memory, e.g. listening to one's favourite soothing CD. may invoke a scene of a sun soaked beach, when the abused felt peaceful and safe.

Also, a grounding exercise,practised at the time of the intimate relationship may help. The patient in their own mind may describe their present environment, in great detail, and who they are with, so as to remind themselves that the re-stimulated emotions are rooted in their traumatic past. This grounding exercise may be learnt and practised in the safety of a therapeutic session.

The counsellor may offer guidance towards healing the painful memories and abuse of trust, to enable sexual activity that is satisfying and pleasant and to overcome the difficult emotions and feelings of trust and intimacy.The therapist may ask open questions that allow for uncensored and detailed feedback from the patient, with guided imagery work e.g. projecting the trauma onto a large screen and observing from a safe distance the "actors" from the trauma.Then, the client imagines she is in the "movie" and playing herself as the victim. This fantasy work I have found to be very difficult for some abused clients and also very cathartic.

Then the patient can reclaim some or all of the power and trust, that was taken from them when abused.

Once the client begins to heal the past traumatic wounds, she may focus on positive goals and aspirations.

The therapist may find the following questions useful in refocusing the client's attention away from the trauma(s). The therapist may ask the patient-

1/ What the client wants from life? e.g. working towards a safe intimate relationship.

2/ What abuse in the past has taken from them and what trusting intimacy may give?

3/ What would they like now? Perhaps an enjoyable partnership or marriage.

4/ Would a support group be helpful? E.g. to trust and be intimate with others.

The answers to the above questions may help the sexually abused client to refocus on the present, and help the patient feel less frightened of an intimate relationship.

To conclude, the sexually abused client may find intimate relations difficult because of her emotional wounds caused by an abuse of power and trust, by the abuser. These wounds may lead to fear, guilt and a sense of powerlessness in intimate relations.

Indeed, it can be difficult for the abused client to avoid restimulation of the actual traumatic incidents. This restimulation may cause flashbacks and lead to self harm, suicidal tendencies, depression and other major mental disorders e.g. schizophrenia, whereby the abused client perceives an inconsistent and uncertain personal reality. The affected may retreat into their own imagery world of delusions and hallucinations. It has to be said that other forms of abuse e.g. emotional , can cause very low self esteem and fear of adult intimacy.Thus, I argue, that low self esteem is a result of sexual abuse and is often followed by a fear of intimacy with adults - making intimate relations difficult or even impossible for some.

The therapist's role is to reframe and refocus the traumas and the "actors" involved by explicit descriptions from the client. This should take place in a safe and trusting practise, with great empathy and absolute positive regard for all the client reveals verbally in sessions. Intimacy difficulties can be overcome by having an agreed goal of promoting high self esteem in the client.Sex abuse is not the end of an enjoyable life, however much one feels it.

Q7.5

<u>People who have been abused are more likely to abuse. True or False?</u>
<u>Discuss and explain your answer.</u>

Firstly what do I mean by abuse? The wounding of another by malpractice or mishandling of a position of power over another. Abuse may be sexual, emotional or physical or one of neglect. I will attempt to answer the question by focusing mostly on sexual and emotional abuse. This does not mean that I believe that physical abuse or neglect are, at times, any less a factor when considering the victims and any causal links between the abused becoming abusers themselves.

Many sexual predators have been abused as children and often by adults that are known to the victim i.e. parent(s), uncles, teachers, scout leaders, priests etc. The trauma of molestation may cause serious mental health issues that may be lifelong conditions, such as schizophrenia and personality disorders. These mental illnesses may be treated by psychiatric medication, e.g. anti-psychotics, and by medium to long term psychotherapy or counselling.

The abused child may grow to accept sexual molestation by adults as a norm and an "acceptable" and "guiltless" form of sexuality in later life. If the victim sees the abuse as the norm and acceptable; he may go on to abuse others as an adult. Just as those who endure corporal punishment at school or home, some may as children see canings and spankings as both "acceptable" and an innocent form of punishment of misdemeanours. This doesn't necessarily mean that spanking children is abusive.

One may argue that shouting and being mentally cruel to young people causes more prolonged psychological damage than spanking and is more likely to cause low self esteem in the child. Spankings may also be abusive, where there is no clear reason for discipline or the victim is subject to naked or semi-naked punishments. It is both physically and sexually abusive in the latter example. Aggression may result from physical abuse and the victim may adopt physical punishments or assaults - later in life.Some young people see corporal punishment as just and relevant to good discipline and suffer no prolonged wounds. It is these well-disciplined young people that grow up healthy and do not go on to abuse others.Where there exists good disciplined children in a loving and protective family environment and clear, safe, recognisable behavioral boundaries - the chastised, verbally or physically, child may not grow up to abuse others.

The child needs to experience a close, warm and natural bonding with their parent(S) and arguably this should involve, especially with boys, forms of "rough housing" or play fighting that encourages trust and confidence in adult relationships. Why boys? Hormonal and societal demands of confident, courageous and protective role models are arguably necessary for a young man to court, hold a financially rewarding job and to be confident in his manhood to love, provide and protect his wife and children. So, a growing boy who receives the aforementioned is less likely to go on to abuse others. The healthy boy has high self esteem and I argue that it is precisely low self esteem that is at the root of most abuse.

Also, there maybe a "tradition" of abuse in a family with several generations of parents encouraging the exploitation and grooming of their offspring. The victims have little or no healthy sexual parents to model or learn from.

However, this is not the same as arguing that genes or hereditary dispositions are acquired. I would argue that science has failed to discover, beyond doubt, a selfish gene and certainly not a paedophilic gene. That is not to say that science may reveal one in the future.

The vulnerable child in the abusive family learns to groom and threaten his victims, with physical beatings or psychological manipulation, so nobody will believe the victim. The abuser is quick to either psychologically blackmail his victim with gifts or threats to his life and well being. The manipulation and grooming with threats or gifts of money, beer, cigarettes etc, are the most common tools used by adult abusers and are used on vulnerable people, just like how the abuser was exploited as a vulnerable minor.

No generalisation can be made concerning the relationship of abused becoming the abuser. Many abused children grow into relatively stable adults and are successful at work, marriage and raising their own children without abuse. Sometimes the abused victim learns what impact abuse has and does not agree with or wish to hurt their own offspring. I argue that many abused victims repress their psychological wounds into their unconsciousness, without awareness that the ego has filtered it out. Often sexual and physical abuse can lead to repressed hurts, leading to the adult victim projecting or transferring their anger onto other suspected paedophiles, rapists and even murderers. Instead of the abused adult acknowledging their own anger, hate or disgust at being assaulted, they may repress their wounded feelings and even persecute harmless, innocent people i.e. scapegoating others for the hurts they endured in childhood.

The repression of the wounds of abuse may be due to fear of the adult abuser: further verbal or physical attacks, rejection and the fear of re-experiencing the unconscious hurts in the conscious mind. The latter may inhibit the abused adult to abuse others, for fear of re-stimulation by conscious awareness of the experience of abuse in possible victims.For example, sights, sounds, touch and smells.

I believe fear plays a major role in paedophilic fantasies and behavior, especially those, as children, who became scared of their parents or other family members. Those young people who have been subject to sexual, physical or emotional abuse over a prolonged period may feel anxious and scared of adult relationships and sex.

Even masturbation may be difficult for the above victims, particularly for children who have been subject to the "Mother Betrayal", where the mother has withdrawn love, nurturing and protection of her son or daughter. Arguably, the father may "betray" his love and protection too. However, the "Betrayal" can cause great adult-to-adult anxiety and low self esteem in the victim.

It is low self esteem that perhaps is at the root of all forms of abuse and without conscious awareness, the victim may turn to being fond of children and to comfort them.Neither is a crime and should not be judged as deviant or perverted. It is whether an individual actually harms a minor that is at the heart of the answer to the question of whether the abused are more likely to abuse others.

Counselling may help the client with low self esteem overcome their wounds and grow in self esteem, even if it takes long-term therapy. Love, empathy and compassion may help the abused to lose their fear of other adults and find adult love and friendship. I believe, that a loved adult with high self esteem is unlikely to go on to abuse another!

Finally, the abused adult may have a powerful inner child in his adult unconsciousness, that can easily identify with young children. Thus enabling the adult "victim" to identify and empathise with the vulnerability and suffering of another young person. Such abused adults with great insight are unlikely to abuse another.

In early childhood an abused client may learn the oppressor-victim-rescuer relationship from the abuser and feel the power of the abuser over him. Rather than feeling the role of helpless victim, the abused may become a teacher or some other child carer and feel the power of the abuser and abuse others. In "helping" children in her care the abuser is acting as a "rescuer", a "victim" and "oppressor" in one role, all of which helps take away the helplessness and powerlessness felt as an abused child. The abuser feels he is taking control of his body and life, in the role just mentioned.

The counsellor may help the abuser by encouraging the abuser to detail the feelings of terror and fear, felt at the time of his abuse. Thus the abuser feels the role of the abused victim and is then able to appreciate what his victim(s) feel and hopefully, by doing so, the abuser may resist abusing in the future.

This does not mean that all abused victims will go on to abuse; given proper care and treatment at the earliest stages of abuse and through sufficient support by a counsellor or peer group sharing it is unlikely the abused will continue to abuse others.

The counsellor can help the abuser, who has been a victim, to understand their feelings as "normal" and to accept, in sexual abusers, that he or she has a adolescent ego state within her that experiences sexual thoughts and fantasies in adulthood. The victim can then begin to see their own sexual imagination as harmless. The therapist will then be able to build up the abuse victim's confidence, self esteem and adequacy as an adult. This understanding of what it feels like for the abused to be molested and their victim's suffering is more likely to result in the abused adult not wanting others to suffer or feel terror at the hands of an abuser. Indeed, the victim may learn to forgive herself and her abusers; through the healing process and wanting to help other victims or abusers themselves.

To conclude and to answer the question directly: there is no empirical evidence of a direct causal relationship between most or all abused victims going on to abuse children. However, there is evidence that many abusers have been abused themselves, as minors, and these young people are more likely to abuse others; particularly as heterosexual men.Also, there is insufficient evidence that abusers inherit "paedophillic" genes from their abusive parents. Most abused children grow up to be law-abiding citizens and enjoy healthy and satisfying consensual adult relationships.

So, I conclude from the arguments above that it is true that some abused young people do develop a disposition to abuse others because of their traumatic ordeals.

But It is false to contend that all abused individuals go on to abuse others as adults.

The answer to this question is not simply "black or white", true or false. It is far more complicated and requires a more empirical based, analytical study, that is far beyond the remit of this writer.

==============================

ASSIGNMENT 8.1

_____

Q.1/ <u>Discuss and explain how you could use the halting protocol.</u>

The halting protocol is a professional tool used by counsellors to delay or prevent destructive behaviour by clients, e.g. self harming and alcohol abuse.

The halting refers to the therapist encouraging his patient to stop and think before she commits a destructive act and think or do something in total contrast to self harming etc. The halting may last as little as 5 seconds to 30 minutes, while the client considers why and what contributed to her wanting to be destructive. The therapist needs to keep the halting to a manageable and achievable time, which may be slowly built upon.

The halting protocol is recommended by the therapist to the client as a means of questioning the patient's automatic actions and reactions, i.e. reactions to hurts and traumas in the past. It is particularly useful for clients with impulsive behaviour redundancies , such as a bulimia sufferer purging herself because she feels too full or fat. It is the counsellor's duty to point out that the patient may continue purging or self harming but the client must await some agreed time before doing so.

A bulimia nervosa client would be asked by the counsellor to stop and consider something completely different to purging, such as looking at a picture of a sunset for 5 seconds and, with practice, up to 10 minutes..
It is unlikely that the Bulimia client would continue purging, after switching attention for a prolonged period. So, the halting starts with a few seconds of reflection to the complete halting of a destructive activity.

The patient unlearns destructive behaviour and learns new ways of reasoning and considering why, for example they purge, and what the possible causes of the destructive behaviour are. Perhaps the client was bullied by her parents or fellow children because she was obese. The cause of eating disorders may be one of feeling "unloved" by her parents and continues into the present where she feels unloved by her partner.

The counsellor should recommending halting, even if the issues surrounding the possible causes are undiscovered or not understood by the patient.

The halting protocol is an essential tool of the therapist for many mental disorders, whereby the therapist encourages the client to find solutions to her destructive behaviour. The patient may temporarily stop and consider her behavior, and finally prevent the harmful behaviour from taking place.

Q8.2/ List ten metaphors for use with clients

Metaphors are another useful therapeutic tool for both counsellors and patients. Metaphors are used by both counsellor and client when it is difficult to invoke a pictorial image in the mind by words and speech, also when emotions and feelings felt by the client are hard to express. These feelings and emotions are easier to express than more direct words. An example of a client who has difficulty in verbalising emotions is the "unloved" patient who feels suicidal and cannot verbalise it.

The client having difficulty in vocalising feelings may find it is too painful to do so. The client may say, "I could just disappear into nothingness." The counsellor would need the necessary skills to understand the metaphors expressed. This metaphor has a clear pictorial image attached and associated with it of feeling unwanted and depressed. A metaphor can carry one word like depression but have many different feelings and emotions applied to it. Depression may feel like emptiness or nothingness to one client and heavy or burdened by another. The meanings are not the same.

Metaphors allow the counsellor or client to elaborate and explore imagery in order to convey information, understanding and perspectives This is extremely useful for both counsellor and client where there is a very hurtful and traumatic cause of depression or BPD. The patient may have been sexually abused and find it difficult to express her deadened emotions and feelings.

The client may bypass normal speech that is direct and self explanatory because she feels vulnerable talking to her male therapist. The client may avoid words that are too difficult to say or verbalize.

.

The therapist may ask her client to symbolise the abuse as an object, such as a black dress, and describe it in detail. I.e. the colours, feel of textures, size, shape etc. The description may convey shared understandings of the abuser and the abused patient. Another metaphor is a movie film where all the actors are talking in a language that the patient cannot understand and where the pictures are disjointed and lack clarity. The therapist may encourage the client to detail the pictures flashing by and the tone of the actors in the movie.

As the patient explores her own metaphors, she may find she begins to interpret the words spoken, as if by the abuser, and the pictures coming together as an understanding of the actual sexual abuse. It is important that the patient stays in control of her own metaphors and imagery, this enables the client to have more control over her feelings and her present reality.

The counsellor may use a dialectical metaphor that has a parallel with the client's own hurtful experience but has a different outcome, to what the client originally experienced during her abuse. The fear of the abuser represented as a "black dress" may be translated into a fierce and angry lion. The lion's anger may well be expressed by the client ,screaming or shouting, which in turn reduces the fear of the abuser.The client feels the power of the abuser and thus regains her own power, that was taken from her during the abuse.. The anger is imagined as directed to the black "dress" abuser, transposed from the rage of the metaphoric lion, acted out by the client. Basically, power returns to the client and is able to re-evaluate the abuser as weak and having no power over her present emotions. It is vital, for client safety, that the client remains in control of her metaphors and actions at all times.

Metaphors for different emotions vary considerably and it is important for therapeutic healing that the therapist understands this.

For example, anger that is repressed or suppressed may be understood by the metaphor as, "simmering below the surface" and anger that is strongly felt as, "feeling like a bull in a china shop". Again, the emotion of anger is the same but experienced differently.

Here are TEN METAPHORS:

1/ "Feeling hot under the collar" (Anger)

2/ " Head is hot" (Anger)

3/ "Mad as a March Hare" (Schizophrenia or Bipolar)

4/ "Being trapped in a black pit" (Depression)

5/ "In an endless black tunnel" (Depression)

6/ "As white as a sheet" (Fear)

7/ "Shaking like a leaf" (Fear)

8/ "Scared to Death" (Fear)

9/ "At a crossroads" (Relationship difficulties or other major decisions)

10/ "Variety is the spice of life" (Joy or happiness)

These metaphors may be used by both counsellor and patient.
The client feels safer using metaphors and less vulnerable emotionally or physically and the counsellor is able to reassure the client that she is safe. Metaphors are vital for better communication and understanding in therapy, where words alone do not suffice in expressing emotions..

Q8.3/

<u>What is the stabilisation process and why is it useful?</u>

Stabilisation is vital for successful counselling and the maximisation of the client's healing in the therapeutic relationship. The therapist needs to ensure that the client's lifestyle and living conditions are not too chaotic, that they prevent the patient from being fully present in the counselling sessions. That means the client is not weighed down by immediate and pressing problems that causes them to not be fully available to therapy.

The patient in a stressful state due to - no fixed address, no access to benefits or income, no access to clean water and food, no shelter, poor sanitation or access to medical care is not ready for counselling.

Home and living conditions of the client need to be secure or stabilised to ensure the client attends sessions regularly, on time, pays the counselling fees appropriately and has enough mindful focus to respond to the counsellor's therapeutic methods.

Before therapy can take place the home and living conditions need to be stabilised with the help of a pro-active counsellor. The therapist's role is to direct the patient to crisis organisations that offer advice with the following:

1/ Secure and maintain regular and adequate housing and disability benefits.

2/ Establish an out of sessions support network of friends, family or carers.

3/ Encourage budgeting and economical lifestyles, e.g. paying bills on time.

4/ Enable repairs, decoration and furnishing of the patient's home.

5/ Support a security of tenure with housing associations, councils or landlord

6/If courts allow it, frequent access to client's children.

7/ Help draw up a crisis plan, for help from social workers, carers, advice lines

8/ Support client's own coping mechanisms , e.g. breathing, mindfulness etc

9/ Establish safe spaces of therapist and client's boundaries, e.g. out of session contact.

Of course, there are limits to what the therapist can help stabilise and much of the above is the responsibility of social workers, community carers, citizens advice workers, benefit advisors and ultimately the client herself.

The stabilisation of the patient's living conditions are necessary, before the therapeutic relationship can be provided for. The stabilisation process means the therapist looks at all aspects of the client's chaotic life which may cause distress or distractions and make therapy difficult.

The client also needs to feel safe from abuse, self harm and addictions, such as substance abuse, alcoholism and access to sharp or hard objects that the patient may use to injure himself. The counsellor needs to make a risk assessment and either remove objects of potential harm or defer counselling until the patient is in a safe place for therapy.

Stabilisation is vitally important for both counsellor and vulnerable clients if they are to fully commit themselves to therapy and out of session factors, such as poor housing, are not to interfere with the success of the healing process in therapy.

The therapist needs to be proactive in stabilising the client's living conditions and stabilisation becomes useful in providing a patient receptive to therapy, feeling safe and secure, fully present and in the right place at the right time for his therapy to be a success.

Q8.4 Why are boundaries essential?

Boundaries are essential for safe professional therapeutic relationships between the counsellor and client. Indeed some would argue that boundaries are essential for the emotional and psychological growth of the patient. Boundaries are about space; safe space for clients, privacy space for counsellors, the practice space, e.g. the structure of the sessions. Boundaries define what is within an agreed boundary and what is outside; this must be agreed upon by client and counsellor at the commencement of sessions. It is the responsibility of the therapist to define and maintain the professional boundaries.

The boundaries basically define acceptable behaviour and conduct in sessions and out of sessions, as well as what is unacceptable conduct in and out of sessions. They are about "rules" of professional behaviour and practice, although most counsellors would not refer to them as such. Anything that would hamper the therapeutic relationship is outside the boundary set by the therapist and must be removed. This is true of unethical issues that affect the trust, clarity, dependency, confidentiality, personal growth, stability, safety etc of the client and counsellor.

Dependency and self reliance are mainly issues regarding the clients, although it is important that the counsellor does not become dependant on the patient for a social life, business affairs or friendship.

The most important factor concerning boundaries is clarity, I.e. being clear and honest about what "rules" govern the limits to the therapeutic relationship.
It is vital that the therapist is transparent and sets the limits or boundaries between herself and the client. The patient who is aware of the boundaries should feel safe and stable enough to learn new therapeutic skills and coping tools. The safety factor may be underlined by a verbal or written contract about the governing boundaries or rules, which is agreed upon by the therapist and client before the counselling begins.

The clarity and clear boundaries are essential or the unethical conduct will undermine the therapeutic relationship and the counsellor will find it difficult to encourage skills that promote the client's independence and self reliance.

Here are some boundaries to be agreed upon between counsellor and client:

1/ No abuse of alcohol, substances or drugs before or during sessions.
2/ No socialising between the therapist and client outside of sessions.
3/ No violence, self harming or attempted suicide during sessions.
4/ No breaking of session durations, place, day, month, fees without consent
5/ No sexual, inappropriate contact or language, e.g. hugging , sexual words
6/ No exploitation, e.g. employing the client

7/ No gossiping, e.g. talking about the client's confessions only to supervisors

8/No hierarchy, e.g. clients as "them" and therapists as the privileged "us"

9/ Honesty and geniuses at all times, e.g. no façade or lying

10/ Privacy, e.g. a soundproof practice, no eavesdropping, anonymity

11/ No judgements or telling by councillor, e.g. no instructing clients

12/ No friendship between client and therapist; no matter the contact time

13/ Maintain professionalism by therapist's objectivity, e.g. no vested interest

14/ Clients as the experts and therapist as a facilitator or guide

15/ The session time belongs to the client and not therapist,

This list is not exhaustive but these boundaries are essential if what is appropriate within and without the counsellor's practice is to be clear to both counsellor and patient. Unethical behaviour is kept out and prevented from causing an unethical therapeutic relationship The safety and security of clients is maintained and ethical professional conduct by the therapist ensures safe therapeutic growth, with the clients undivided attention and the successful learning of skills and coping.

Q8.5/

What is grounding?

Grounding refers to feeling safe and emotionally stable in the here and now. Being grounded in the psychological sense is encouraged by counsellors as a means to be present and to be aware of one's body, mind and environment. For example, a volatile schizophrenic who suffers from delusions and hallucinations is not grounded because of their lack of awareness of "reality".

It can be said that one who is volatile is subject to extreme changes in mood and emotions, or arguably one who is unaware of their natural world and are not grounded. Grounding then refers to being aware of one's thoughts, feelings, emotions, physical body and nature in the now.

The counsellor's role is to reduce the distress and hallucinations of her patients by encouraging self awareness and using mindful skills to keep the patient in the present. The client is stabilised by mindful walking or breathing, this helps the client to be in the present surroundings and the moment of now. Where the negative and distressful state of mind and experiences cannot be stopped, the therapist works on reducing the impact of delusions, hallucinations, flashbacks, thoughts, feelings, emotions and moods Grounding helps the patient to be less swamped or overwhelmed by the aforementioned hallucinations, flashbacks etc from the past abuses and traumas in their lives and to feel safe and in control of themselves and their behaviour.

The following methods and skills can be encouraged by the counsellor, for the patient to use when distressed or for to practice when well:

A safe place

The therapist asks the patient to think of a safe and secure place where they can go, in their mind, when feeling distressed. The counsellor asks the client to describe in detail this totally safe and happy place and ask them what they can take from it, e.g. what it feels like to be totally safe and protected. The counsellor then asks the client if they can go there in times of distress.

A Transactional Object

This refers to an object that belongs to a safe and pleasant time and place from the past, which reminds the client of safety and calmness; it could be a shell from a beautiful beach or a comfort blanket from childhood.
These examples may relate to feeling safe and protected, when the client is feeling stressed or unhappy. The physical object, which reminds the client of warm memories and happiness, may be small and can be carried about. The object is grounding the patient , through memory, in the present moment of restimulated safety and peace with her environment.

Breathing

The counsellor may ground the patient by encouraging mindful breathing exercises, which can be done alone when distressed or with the therapist's guidance. The therapist asks the patient to take and follow slow, rhythmic, deep breathes down into her abdomen and filling the lungs. The client may imagine the air slowly entering the client's nose or mouth and filling her entire body from toe to her head. The mindful breathing may be done for 5 seconds to begin with and for an initial 10 times, until the patient feels confident to increase the breathing 20 more times. In times where fear or terror is being experienced and there is a sense of urgency, the patient may take a slow deep breath and then breath out fast. The slow, then fast breathing out method can induce a smile or laughter. The client may hold a transactional object, like a shell, at the same time to feel safe and more grounded in herself.

Mindfulness

The therapist may ask the client to picture a stream in the patient's mind and , with closed eyes, imagine leaves or small pieces of paper with a thought or emotion attached to it, flowing down the stream out of sight.
The negative thoughts and emotions on the paper or leaves disappear too. The therapist asks how this feels to the client as her negative feelings float away. This exercise can be accompanied by slow, deep breathing and with an object, like the sea shell, held in the hand. The negative thoughts and feelings are disposed of and the client is grounded by breathing.

This method is extremely useful for hallucinations and flashbacks from the past , as the mindful exercise brings the client back into the present and away from past distress or abuse.

Mindful Walking

This is another grounding tool. The therapist may ask the patient to walk slowly and calmly around the room, with the client's attention totally on the contact with the feat on the ground. The counsellor encourages the client to be aware of the sensations of the feet, as she slowly walks around the room. The therapist asks the client to count up to ten steps and increase the number as the client feels more confident. The client then may feel grounded in herself, bodily, and her awareness centred in the present.

Again, the patient may complement this method with breathing slowly and carrying a transactional object with her.

Grounding Statements

A grounding statement may include writing on a card, detailing the name, address, age and the names of the client's partner , children and pets.

 This "flashcard" is portable on a small piece of card and reminds the patient of their identity and where they live, especially if they are confused by delusions, hallucinations etc and unsure of who they are. It is useful too in reminding the client that a stressful, abusive or traumatic event is not happening now and that they are a capable adult grounded by their name and location. The "flashcard" helps remind the distressed client of themselves and their surroundings; thus stabilising the patient in the present now.

The flashcard may be copied onto a poster and using comforting colours, it may be placed on a private wall in the client's home. The client may read the flash poster whenever experiencing flashbacks, hallucinations etc.

Using warm colours the patient may also write up on a poster the following:
1/ "This too shall pass"
2/ "I have real thoughts not reality thoughts"
3/ " I am an adult now aged…"
4/ "I am safe and secure now"

The above statements will help remind the patient that she is no longer being bullied or abused and that she is grounded in the safe here and now.

Finally, other grounding techniques that a counsellor can suggest to a client:

1/ Sing along or dance to a piece of favourite music that makes one feel happier.

2/ When angry stamp hard as one walks around a room

3/ Make eye contact with oneself in a mirror or with a close friend

4/ Look, listen or feel the texture of an object, e.g. a ticking clock.

5/ Describe a beautiful photograph of the mountains, trees, sea, animals etc.

6/Light a fragrant candle or incense and watch and smell the smoke

7/ Wear worry beads or a pearly necklace and count them when anxious

Grounding is then one of being fully in the here and now, free from memories of past traumas and abuse, away from feeling confused about one's identity due to flashbacks, hallucinations that are visual or auditory, deluded thoughts or perceptions. Grounding is any method or technique that takes away focusing on the past memories and grounds the client in the safe, calm present: the moment of now. Grounding is a useful tool for therapists to apply as therapy for any mental disorder from anxiety to depression; wherever and whenever the patient is not fully aware of the present moment or is not stabilised.

===========================

ASSIGNMENT 9

_____

<u>Describe and explain the process for treating someone with depression.</u>

The first objective of the therapist when confronted by someone complaining of depression is to assess whether the patient is in immediate danger or risk to themselves or others. The counsellor may ask the client, "Do you feel suicidal?", " Do you want to die?", "Have you any plans to commit suicide?", "Do you have any weapons, poisons, pills etc to commit suicide?", "Do you feel energetic?" Energy levels have to be high enough to act out suicide and if the answer is "yes" to the other questions, then it is not counselling that is immediately necessary but admission to a psychiatric unit by a referral to a psychiatrist or the Emergency services. It could be a matter of life or death and the client will need to be stabilised enough to undergo counselling.

Next, ask the full name, address, contact telephone number, next of kin's details in case of emergency, GP's name and Psychiatrist, if applicable, name and contact details. The therapist should ask the client which psychiatric and general medication he is on and the relevant dosages. The therapist needs also needs to be aware of the client's diagnoses, such as Bipolar 1 or Major Depressive Disorder, in able to deal with the presenting symptoms. If the client has a depressive disorder of any kind then psychiatric medication should be considered by a referral to his GP or Psychiatrist. Apart from non-clinical "blues", the treatment of depression should be a multi-party approach with psychiatrists, GP, and carers or, in the case of a child - a social worker.

The next question to ask the client is whether he has a history of depression or a history of mental illness in the family. Someone with a history of mental illness is far more likely to suffer depression again, compared to the wider public.

If there is a history of suicide in the family or by the patient, then the client is assessed as more at risk from killing themselves. Sometimes clients may copy suicidal or depressive behaviour by close relations, rather than an illness inherited in the genes.

A history of psychiatric care may include in-patient care in a psychiatric unit, a "therapeutic community" , a "halfway house" or if a young person - a care home. The patient maybe attending a psychiatrist's outpatient surgery and considered well enough to stay at home. A community psychiatric nurse or social worker may counsel the client and deliver medication to the patient's home.

The therapist needs to assess how much the patient is at risk from suicide, as this is one of the most common effects of depression and needs to be assessed by the therapist to avoid tragedies occurring. Factors that should be taken very seriously by the counsellor are the patient storing medicines, tidying up affairs, making a premature will, letting friends or family aware of her suicidal feelings etc. The counsellor may need to report these factors to her supervisor or to other health professionals, e.g. NHS Psychologists, Psychiatrists or a social worker.

.

The counsellor needs to get a clearer picture of the client's risk of suicide and will need to have some understanding of the moderate to severe levels of depression.

Everyone has the blues from time to time, a non-clinical, short lived low mood, which may be a reaction to a stressful event or for no particular reason at all. If the client has the "blues", then no medication need to be prescribed and counselling over a few weeks may prove more beneficial to the client. Simply exploring the feelings around the event that triggered the "blues".

Here is a brief mention of the types of depression and their relation to suicide:

1/ Major Depressive Episode

A depressed mood that lasts most of the day and every day. It may be diagnosed as endogenous depression or by a colour, as described by the British Holistic Medical Association (BHMA) . It may be Grey or Black.

If Grey, there is energy sufficient to carry out a suicide but little will to do so.

If Black, there is little hope but little will power or energy to attempt suicide but suicidal thoughts are usually frequent.

2/ Mixed Episode

A Manic and Major Depressive Episode, with Black or Psychotic depression.

3/ Major Depressive Disorder

Two or more episodes of Major Depression, with Grey or Black energy levels.

4/ Dysthymic Disorder

Depression that lasts most of the day for 2 years or more, with Grey energy.

5/ Bipolar Disorder 1 and 2

At least 1 manic and 1 depressive mood, lasting for a few days, months or even hours for each swing in mood. The client will feel euphoric or "high" in mania and depressed enough to interfere with daily routines and work. This illness often lasts many years but responds well to counselling. "Lack of Sparkle to Black in energy levels.

6/ Cyclothymiacs Disorder

This lasts for at least 2 years with mania and depressive symptoms but no major depressive disorder, Grey or Black energy levels.

Depression is a prolonged low mood of sadness, emptiness, often with hopelessness, helplessness, negative thinking, reduced will power and the threat of suicide. However, as seen, its effects vary widely from one diagnoses to another and any assessment should be kept in the mind of the counsellor.

The different suicide risk factors, as described above, can be assessed and responded to by the counsellor and mental health team. The details of the above may be obtained from the health carers or ,if possible, from the client himself. Finally, the diagnosis above may be referred back to the psychiatrist or GP. How then can the risk of suicide be formally kept out of therapy? A contract with the client, child's parent or guardian is one method.

A verbal or written contract is vital if boundaries are to be made clear and kept to, as well as identifying what is allowed "IN" and "OUT" of the therapeutic relationship. The contract is between the counsellor and patient or guardian.

Firstly, the therapist should state in the agreed contract that no suicidal attempts or self harming should be attempted while undergoing therapy. In the case of BPD and those with "Black" depressions, self harm may be the only way of preventing death and should not be discouraged in such cases.

Secondly, the structure of therapy sessions must be made clear in the agreed contract. The duration of each session is around 45 to 50 minutes, once per week or month, for an agreed initial period of possibly 8 to 12 weeks.

The payment of the counsellor's fees, when, how much etc, need to be agreed before the commencement of counselling and if cancellation fees are imposed or waived, if at least 24 hours are given by therapist or client. Arguably in cases of emergencies or patient's unstable state of mind, e.g. suicidal depression, some therapists may not charge for a missed session. This is an ethical decision and may not apply to those counsellors working for a supervisory body, e.g. the NHS. A private practice may also allow for reduced fees for those on limited income, e.g. sickness benefits. The ethical code of practice of the counsellor's governing body should be consulted e.g. the BACP.

The agreed contract must establish firm rules on boundaries governing a , " safe place" for the therapist and client to work in, e.g. privacy and client confidentiality, including "client's space" for the patient to understand that it is primarily the client's time and not the therapist's.

This means that the client is free to talk about anything he chooses in the sessions and it is not the time for the counsellor to chat about his favourite TV show or holiday etc.The "therapist's space" equally is for the counsellor and his privacy and his right to be uninterrupted out of session time needs to be respected by the patient.

Contracts agreed by client and therapist are essential for safe counselling, safe and ethical boundaries, statements of limitations on the therapeutic relationship, and foremost for the physical and mental welfare of the client.

.

It is not only boundaries that create the conditions for good counselling but a plan or model that includes stabilisation of the client's living and social conditions. A patient cannot be ready for counselling if his personal life is so chaotic that he is overwhelmed by distractions and problems. The counsellor should be proactive in directing the client to the relevant local housing authority concerning; housing benefits, finding living accommodation , ensuring proper repairs of the house or flat and a support network. This support network might include a social life with friends and family, or practical help from a social worker or a CPN e.g. help with mobility or moving into a new home. Thus, aiding the stabilisation of a client who will be better equipped to learn new coping skills and a greater understanding of his illness.

A brief stay in a psychiatric unit may also help stabilise the client and help the patient to break through black depression: relief from the numbness or agitation that depression brings and free up the consciousness for counselling. Also, the client may break the cycle of performing, failing, becoming depressed and more failures due to increased stress.
A hospital or children's' care home may act as a sanctuary for those clients facing seemingly hopeless and insolvable personal issues, e.g. holding down a job or a minor facing parental neglect.

If the client is prescribed antidepressants by a psychiatrist in hospital, then the patient's response or recovery may be monitored. The patient's home may not be a good enough place to try out new medication due to adverse effects, e.g. the pills may fail to deal with symptoms and lead to suicidal feelings.

If the client lives alone it would be almost impossible for a counsellor to know if the medication is helping or if the patient is taking medication regularly. A CPN may monitor the client on new antidepressants but the visits may not be frequent enough.

A hospital may prevent suicidal depressive behaviour and if the client fails to respond to the multitude of antidepressants, and ECT maybe an option. Some clients with black or psychotic depressions have benefited from ECT but it does raise many ethical issues, such as the morality of slamming 100 volts of electricity through the client's brain. It should therefore be avoided completely or used as a final resort, when all other psychiatric, psychological methods have been adopted.

The other problem of hospitalisation, before psychotherapy, is that it tends to foster passivity among the in-patients. The psychiatric team have a very difficult task of providing comfort, safety and treatment while helping the client to act more independent and be self reliant.

A short stay in a unit or a referral to a "halfway" house may encourage more independent living, at the same time as applying psychiatric therapy. But, there is a tendency for patients to simply sit back and take the tablets, without helping themselves to recover from depression. When this arises the psychiatric team should assess whether the client is ready and able to undertake psychotherapy.

Depression does not have to be a life sentence and the counsellor should challenge the client, as to their responsibilities and mental strengths, e.g. living away from parents and trusting their own wisdom and intuition.

Once the client has been stabilised on medication or by changing poor living conditions, then counselling may commence. The therapist may follow the "Inner Child" or Transactional Analysis method, where the counsellor explains the Parent, Adult and Child ego states. This model is especially useful for depressives of all kinds because a depressed client has an unhappy inner child.

The client is more able to cope with suicidal features by strengthening the inner child and adult ego states together e.g. the adult state can love and reassure the distressed inner child"Flashbacks" and hallucinations are diminished as the inner child feels safer, protected, unconditionally accepted and loved i.e. by the stronger adult ego state.The premise being that flashbacks, delusions and hallucinations are rooted in fear; located in the child ego state.

The strong adult/child bonding, encouraged by the counsellor, can be a constant resource in difficult or critical times, e.g. dealing with past sexual abuse or other childhood traumas, such as the "Mother Betrayal".

The therapist may use swapping chairs or writing hands, as representing the child, adult or parent ego states. The counsellor may ask the patient when he first became depressed and discovers it occurred after his Mother stopped loving him abruptly, due to his father continually moaning and criticising the client's mother. Early depressive symptoms, in the hypothetical client, may have began to emerge at the age of 12 years, such as tearfulness, headaches, fear and anxiety.

The therapist requests the client to sit in the "father's" chair and use the real father's nagging. Then, the client moves to the "child's" chair and is asked by the therapist to respond verbally to his father's demands. The switching chairs between "father", "mother" and "child" continues, possibly over weeks or months until the mute depression turns to cathartic emotional release, e.g. anger, rage and trembling in fear. The therapist asks the patient to use a rolled up newspaper to hit the "Parent" chair with, if rage occurs.

Another tool used by the therapist is to ask the angry child to write an uncensored letter to his mother and father (Parent state) expressing in vivid detail as to how he felt about the "betrayal of love" and his father's critical stance. The client is less likely to be suffering black depressions, after the Inner Child work.

Finally, the model of telephone counselling may be used by the counsellor, as it has some aspects of face-to-face counselling, e.g. the client is able to express thoughts and feelings in a safe therapeutic relationship.

The duration of time may be the same as facial contact with a session lasting 50 minutes and as regular as once per week or monthly. Privacy and confidentiality is maintained with the client and the therapist having physical anonymity. There is no travelling involved, so a client may choose a telephone counsellor who specialises in the client's favoured therapeutic model, e.g. DBT, CBT, TA etc. This form of therapy is ideal for those who have busy lifestyles or who may live in remote areas.

The client may be physically disabled, lacking in energy due to black depression or housebound without access to frequent public transport.
In effect, the counsellor comes to the client's house by the telephone. The therapeutic benefits are the client may feel free to talk about more private topics that she would be unable to talk openly about with a practice based therapist.

However, the client has to be careful not to say anything that takes her out of her comfort zone, after revealing her deepest secrets to her counsellor. It may be difficult and embarrassing feeling she may have risked being judged by the therapist and she may fear rejection. Also, there are no physical body language clues for the client to interpret or facial expressions, e.g. frowning, to divert her attention away from the conversation. Equally, the therapist has to recognise the patient's tone of voice and long pauses to suggest the scale of depression, e.g. a very soft or low voice and inability to give answers to the therapist's questions may reveal a state of depression.

The therapist may request the client practices the Inner Child work at home, where the patient feels safe and without worries of not performing properly for the counsellor. I.e. not trying to impress the counsellor.

Inner Child and telephone counselling are part of the overall model, including stabilisation of living conditions, medication, psychiatric care for some depressives. It has to be said that those whom are suffering from moderate grey depression may not need any form of stabilisation or psychiatric care and may be ready to commence psychotherapy anytime, after assessment by the counsellor.

Inner child work would need to be reviewed both subjectively and objectively, from time to time, just like any other form of psychotherapy. The easiest way to review counselling and to establish how effective it has been, would be for the counsellor to ask the client directly how does he feel about his therapy and whether he finds the techniques helpful.

At the end of each session or, if not too invasive, immediate feedback may easily be done over the telephone on as-you-go basis, such as asking the client every few minutes during the sessions. The therapist can also ask for feedback on his approach from his supervisor, at least once a month. The counsellor may take regular notes during the session, to be reviewed between sessions to see how effective his methods have been and what progress has been made by the client. The reviewing of notes should be weekly or monthly, depending on how frequently the therapist talks to his patient and supervisor.

The counsellor and client may keep a diary to record and review their daily feelings and behaviour. The client can see how much progress has been done towards the goal of "loss of sparkle" or "gold"; where no depressive symptoms exist. Some depressives such as those with BPD or Bipolar may have a biological cycle that is unlikely to disappear altogether. The client's diary may elucidate suicide attempts or ideation, self harming, mood changes and the success or failure of different techniques. Once the therapist has read or heard what is in the patient's diary, he may review his methods and techniques to increase effectiveness.

The counsellor's review of the client's diary may take place every session; weekly, monthly or quarterly, depending on the severity of the depression and to maintain good therapeutic practice. Someone with suicidal depression may need weekly reviews, whereas a patient with Dysthymic Disorder with few, if any, suicidal thoughts may only require a monthly or quarterly review by the therapist.

A more objective form of formal reviewing would be between a qualified supervisor and the counsellor. The therapist would need to send his notes concerning the treatment of his clients, at least monthly to his supervisor. The supervisor is able to listen, reflect and offer a critical review of the counsellor's work and suggest alternative techniques or tools that may be more effective in helping a depressive. The supervisor can also review professional codes of ethical practice and ensure they are being maintained.

A supervisor should review the therapist's work for up to 1 and a half hours, every month; this can be done over the telephone or face-to-face.

Finally, the therapist may send reviews to the client's psychiatrist or GP, if requested by the doctor. The counsellor may initiate the formal review of his client to a doctor, if he feels "out of his depth", or if the client's health is life threatening. The review may take place very occasionally or more frequently, if the counsellor is working as part of a NHS Psychiatric or Child Protection team. The therapist needs to maintain confidentiality by requesting permission from the client to reveal personal information revealed in sessions. However, if the patient has or is about to kill herself then confidentiality may be broken.

Reviewing, informal or formal, is a good means to see how the client is coping and whether the counsellor's techniques are effective. But, how do we really know if the therapy has worked?

The simplest method that the counsellor may use to establish whether his therapeutic methods have worked is to ask the client , in an open question, is "how are you feeling now?" The therapist puts no pressure on the client to say a definite "yes" or "no", if the counsellor asks an open question as to whether the patient feels depressed. The client replying "yes" to an open question may feel a sense of failing on his part and this may cause further stress and even greater depression. If the client replies with saying, "I am happy", " I am feeling good", " I feel energetic" etc; then the client is obviously not depressed or less depressed than normal. This assumes the client is not disguising her depression, because of a need to perform and impress the counsellor.

The therapist may check the authenticity of the non-depressed claims of the client, by listening carefully to the client's tone of voice or body language in "face-to-face" sessions.

If the client sounds non-responsive or is looking down to the floor and avoiding eye contact with the counsellor, whilst saying she is not depressed, then the tone or body language may reveal otherwise.

Another subjective technique used by the counsellor might be to ask the client to contradict an unhappy statement, by pretending to laugh or simply smile; to encourage cathartic release. In using Inner Child work there maybe misunderstandings about what the Parent, Adult and Child ego states represent and this will need to be clarified by the therapist, as a client without depression is arguably one whom has a healthy adult-child state relationship.

A more objective analysis that may be utilised by the counsellor is "scaling", where the client has to meet certain criteria on a continuum from, for example, 10 to 100: Ten being psychotic depression to 100 enjoying healthy psychological functioning.

It is safe to say that the counsellor's therapy has worked, if symptoms of depression are diminishing or disappearing. This is especially true if over a period of weeks or months, a client who has been on a high dose of antidepressants comes to the therapist for counselling with suicidal or self harm symptoms. One may say that the counselling has worked if the client. begins to lower her daily dose of medication; with the consent of the psychiatrist and the client begins to stop self destructive tendencies.

The client may feel well enough to discontinue therapy or meet with her counsellor less frequently, but there may be other reasons for sessions ending, e.g. family, school or work commitments , and the counsellor needs to discuss endings thoroughly with his patient.

The client may well be referred to her GP by the counsellor to clinically decide formally if the depressive illness has lessened. A counsellor may receive a report, on the progress of his client,from the GP or psychiatrist.

The counsellor may clarify the wellness of his client by checking the following criteria for signs of diminishing depression and to establish whether his therapy has worked:

1/ NO difficulties in falling asleep.

2/ NO waking early or oversleeping

3/ NO enduring tearfulness or prolonged sadness

4/ NO under or over eating

5/ NO major increase or decrease in body weight

6/ Improved concentration and self awareness or mindfulness

7/ NO regular thoughts about death or suicide

8/ Increased interest in people or more active social life

9/ Increased energy levels, enabling client to carry out daily duties.

10/ NO restlessness or prolonged inactivity, e.g. pacing the floor or lying prostrate on a bed or couch.

Finally, the less depressed client may be more able to be cathartic, and feel or express her repressed emotions, and break out of the black pit of depression; feeling alive and with a genuine interest in life.

Assessment of client

NAME: Angela Jones   NEXT OF KIN: Trevor Jones

ADDRESS: The cottage,

Rose Lane,

Salcombe,

Devon.   SOCIAL WORKER: none

ASSESSED BY: Francis Sturt BSc

D.O.B. 03/ 12/ 1964

GP: Dr. Boyd TEL: 01472 123456

CONSULTANT: Dr. Redwell TEL:02674 789321

As the client's therapist, what does the client feel I can provide?

Client feels I can help her cope with the depression and suicidal thoughts she feels and stop her from self harm.

What are the client's expectations regarding therapy?

Client wants me to listen carefully to her and give her good coping methods and skills.

What do you feel she needs?

Client needs lots of practical ideas and empathy from me. Just someone who cares about her and her depression.

<u>What do you identify as the client's main problems?</u>

Bipolar Disorder, anxiety, terror, social phobia.

<u>Give details of previous psychiatric history:</u>

Diagnosed with reactive depression in 1989 and Bi-Polar in 2001
Admitted to a psychiatric unit in 2002, following a breakdown.

<u>Does she have any criminal convictions / cautions?</u> NONE

<u>State details of client's current medication:</u>
Lithium 100 mg Parstelin 300mg

<u>Give details of client's mood, ways of coping and beliefs:</u>

Client's mood is one of black depression,most of the day, and of being very high in the afternoons.
Client copes by going to a Gym and walking everywhere.

<u>Please give details of any substance abuse, drug taking and alcohol use</u>:
Client is a heavy vodka, social drinker.

<u>Please detail client's present feelings:</u> guilt, hopelessness, suicidal, helplessness, will power and energy levels:

Client has very little energy. She feels suicidal every day but no energy to do act on her suicidal feelings.Client feels totally hopeless and helpless.

Please list details of delusions, hallucinations and flashbacks:
Only "flashbacks" to childhood abuse.

Client's ability to concentrate, attention and memory: Client cannot concentrate on anything for more than 10 minutes and can only remember hurtful times.

Detail client's self esteem, confidence and ability to perform:
Client hasn't any confidence or self esteem; she hates herself.

Give details of client's risk of suicide:
Client feels suicidal most days but doesn't feel like harming anyone.

Is the client receiving help from CPN's, social workers etc?
No, only from her mother and her husband: Trevor.

Any additional confidential information and details of other contacts; carers, family, teachers etc:
Client sometimes flashes bibles at vicars, although she is not religious.

Details of any history of mental disorders in family: NONE

Dated: Signed:

This is a contract for psychotherapy between Angela Jones (client) and Francis Sturt.(Psychotherapist).

Please tick each box, against each statement, client agrees with or leave blank if client disagrees.

1/ To inform the emergency services if the client is in danger. Dial "999" for an ambulance, if the client has self harmed or attempted suicide.[]

2/ To break client's confidentiality if the client is being abused. If this is in the best interests of the client or required by law.[]

3/ NO violence, self harm or suicidal attempts during sessions. ,e.g. physical attacks on therapist, cutting arms, taking an overdose.[]

4/ To report sexual or physical abuse to the police or social workers. Especially where the law demands it and it is in the best interests of the abused.[]

5/ To receive undivided attention from the therapist during sessions., e.g. to be totally "there" for the client without distractions, such as noises or distracting thoughts. []

6/ To encourage self reliance and independent living, e.g. less dependency on the psychiatric services, and living alone or in a "halfway house." Also, less medication and contact with social workers, CPN's etc, if possible.[]

7/ A diary to be kept by the client to report any traumatic or other important events, e.g. to give details of how well the client is coping during out of session time and to report the details back to the counsellor. The therapist may modify his therapy, depending on how well his tools and skills are being used by clients.[]

8/ Notes will be taken at times by the therapist during sessions., these should be brief and state important facts only, e.g. self harm or depression. Avoid lengthy notes, as one may miss an important point, when note taking during sessions e.g. suicidal thoughts. These notes should be sent to the supervisor.[]

9/ To have a "crisis" plan , when in danger, to confide in a friend or dial a helpline, e.g. have a packed bag ready when the client or the client's child are being abused. Go to a refuge or a friend's house for a few days. Contact social workers for child protection, or phone a helpline, such as NDVH or the NSPCC.[]

10/ No abuse of alcohol, drugs or substances during or just before sessions. This will interfere with the client's attention and make them non-responsive to therapy., e.g. volatile.[]

11/ NO inappropriate touching or sexually suggestive talk during sessions. This may cause distress and "flashbacks" in abused clients.[]

12/ NO invasion of privacy by relations, parents or partners during sessions. No eavesdropping, using a shared line, or interruption of the sessions, as this may cause the therapist to be distracted and lose his attention on what is being said by clients. Parents and Partners may have a vested interest in the outcome of the therapeutic session., e.g. not to be seen as the abuser, in the case of alleged abuse by a client.[]

13/ NO sworn statements of secrecy by counsellor. This is vital as the law may require disclosure of client's notes and statements, especially where abuse or terrorism applies. The counsellor has to forward notes to his supervisor and disclosure may be in the best interests of the client or children.[]

14/ NO judgements by therapist on the behaviour or opinions of the client's family or friends. The therapist may have a vested interest in maintaining a moral position, that the relations and friends of the client do not share., e.g. their alcohol "abuse" causes addiction and encourages violence to his client.[]

15/ NO displays of shock or revulsion at the client's revelations and experiences. This may distance the therapist from the client: " I'm a really bad and helpless case."[]

16/ NO dishonest statements or behaviour by counsellor. It is important for the client's safety and well being that they feel able to trust the therapist's analysis and actions, if the client is to be healed or helped.[]

17/ NO condemnation of client's thoughts, feelings or behaviour. No judgements, as this may inhibit the client to speak openly about his concerns and problems. The client needs to feel valued and accepted for emotional growth to take place, otherwise the client may dismiss the therapist entirely and doubt his diagnoses and techniques.[]

18/ NO friendship or social activities between therapist and client, e.g. No chats over coffee in a café or a game of squash together, as this will damage the objectivity of the therapist, e.g. the therapist may discourage the client's friendships with others, as he has a subjective view of who is suitable for his "friend" client.[]

19/ NO exploitation by counsellor of client, especially regarding financial payments for services offered by a counsellor. No employment of clients, business partnerships, cash loans, gifts etc. This may damage objectivity of the therapist , as it changes the client-therapist relationship and is unethical.[]

20/ To give notice, by either party, of charges and changes of fees . The payment of fees should be clear from the beginning of therapy and when and how much is payable. Most qualified counsellors charge at least £35 per 50 minute session and this is usually reviewed annually, with the therapist giving at least a month's notice of any fee changes to the client. []

21/The therapist should give as much notice as possible if he intends to take a holiday, attend a workshop, training etc. At least a week plus one week, if sessions are weekly; a month plus one month, if the sessions are monthly etc.

The client should not be charged for cancellations of sessions made by the counsellor, unless the therapist has provided several alternative dates for the client. The therapist must give as much notice as possible or the client may feel abandoned.

Likewise, the client should give notice of hospitalisation, or fees may be payable regardless of client's circumstances. In any case the client should give at least 24 hours notice of cancellation. The therapist may be ethically bound to waive fees, if the patient is admitted to inpatient care, in an emergency e.g. a suicide attempt.

The therapist is offering a "valuable" service to the client, of a life worth living, and in private practice it is his usually the counsellor's only means of income. It is morally right that fees are payable by the client for all sessions until the end of treatment.[]

22/ If the therapist terminates the therapy he should offer alternative help to those clients who require it, e.g. a psychiatrist, psychologist or another therapist. This "ending" requires as much notice as possible, a week plus a week for weekly sessions etc, otherwise the client may feel unready or abandoned by the therapist. The counsellor can prevent any sense of the client feeling "abandoned", if both counsellor and client mutually agree to the ending of therapy, e.g. when the therapeutic approach is deemed unsuitable and it has reached its useful limits and is proving non-productive, for the patient. []

If you have not ticked some of the boxes above, please give your reasons and the client's disagreements below.

I agree that my above answers are true and accurate, signed:

==

Assignment 10

_____

A CBT/ Integrative Programme for a Hypothetical Client (Fully Revised)
By Francis R Sturt

Katie is a hypothetical client that has sought counselling for mental health and psychological disorders.

Description of disorder, including relevant physiology and clinical treatment.

Katie suffers from unipolar depression with no displays of mania or euphoria. Katie also self-harms her body and has suicidal tendencies. She cuts her arms and legs frequently and has been admitted to hospital Casualty departments as an outpatient for treatment of her self harming. Katie's depression manifests itself as one of feeling sad, lonely, withdrawn with irrational guilt, resentment, outbursts of anger, tearfulness, and persistent low mood with suicidal ideation.

Katie also has panic attacks, when she sweats, feels intense fear without an obvious cause, trembles, hyperventilates and releases excessive noradrenaline in the brain and this activates her flight and fright response. Katie's Sympathetic Nervous System is activated and leads to irregular heartbeat, high blood pressure, increase in oxygen, blood clotting, lack of appetite, a high temperature, slow digestion and a poor flow of blood to her bodily extremities, i.e. hands and feet.

This in turn causes her Parasympathetic Nervous System to be activated to restore homeostasis, leading to increased digestive activity; carbon dioxide inhalation which reduces her hyperventilation; an increase in faster thinking; less profusion of sweat, with a decrease in shaking and trembling. Katie has suffered from depression since her early teens and all of her adult life. The causes can be traced back to her infancy, when she was emotionally and sexually abused by her father.

Katie first contacted NHS Direct at the age of 20 years, concerning her self harming, which had become very serious. Katie was recommended to consult her GP at her nearby local surgery and. after 2 visits she was diagnosed with having depression and prescribed anti-depressants. Katie was instructed to take her medicine twice a day but she failed to do so. Consequently Katie severely self harmed and was sent to her hospital casualty department for cuts to her arms and legs.

Katie saw her GP, upon discharge from hospital, and her anti-depressants were increased. Katie now took her medication regularly and also attended an appointment with a consultant psychiatrist. The consultant referred her to in-patient care at the Doncaster Mental Health Unit. Katie was prescribed tranquillisers with her anti-depressants for her suicidal depression and social anxiety.

Next, Katie was assigned a community social worker who helped her to live more independently in a shared NHS community care hostel for women with mental and domestic problems. Katie received care from community psychiatric nurses and is now in a stable but serious condition. She has to be routinely monitored for self harm and suicidal tendencies.

The self harm and risk of suicide greatly reduced after a few weeks, probably due to her living away from her abusive and argumentative parents.

Assessment criteria and plan of action.

_____

As a counsellor I saw Katie for the first time, when recommended by her GP. Katie had been discharged from the women's' hostel, at the age of 24. Initially I took down details of her clinical and personal history, including school and family life experiences. Katie will be asked to answer a General Health Questionnaire and from this I helped form my own diagnoses of depression and panic attacks due to social phobia. The criteria Katie will have to meet is whether she has suffered from depression for at least 2 weeks, all day, everyday, to establish whether Katie has major unipolar depression without manic episodes.

The depression diagnosis will be met if Katie shows symptoms of lethargy, false guilt, persistent low mood, a lack of interest in hobbies and day to day chores, e.g. washing and dressing herself appropriately. I will also need to take into consideration environmental factors such as adequate accommodation, diet, work, mobility, education and the level of daily care by parents and the psychiatric care team.

I will need to take into consideration Katie's history of emotional and sexual abuse from her infancy. As a result of her abuse Katie may feel hate, rage and anger towards her abusive father and this may have been repressed, leading to more generalized anger and depression, which Katie feels unable to direct to her father in an appropriate, assertive way.

The repressed anger and fearful experiences may cause flashbacks, prompted by smells, sights and sounds that result in nightmares. The re-stimulation of past neglect by present events may induce such unbearable mental pain that she becomes avoidant and withdraws from contact with her parents, usually to her bedroom where she feels safer and more in control of such events. Thus Katie imprisons herself and is alone most of every day accompanied by depression and phobias of what is out "there" and fears defenceless and vulnerable to attacks from men. Katie's parents have seemingly betrayed her love and protection at an early age. So Katie feels both betrayed and neglected, which causes her to blame herself, as she feels "responsible" and "guilty" and self harms to punish herself as it must be her "fault". Thus increasing her depression and self harm.

Initially we will need to establish a collaborative relationship with Katie sharing all major decisions regarding her counselling. The plan, which may be reviewed depending on her progress, is to reduce the depressive episodes, self harm and phobias. The initial period will be approximately 6 months and reviewed at the end of that period. The aim is to maintain a constructive relationship with all clinical professionals, nurses, social workers and other charitable bodies involved.

The plan will involve raising Katie's self awareness and self management of her own mental health disorder symptoms.

.

The overall goals are to apply CBT techniques and skills in sessions, reduce the episodic panic attacks and her high levels of depression, thus allowing for less dependency on medication, create greater awareness of her condition and appropriate coping strategies and to replace self harming with less destructive and safer methods of controlling inward aggression and alleviation of suicidal temptations. It must be said that I will not suggest to Katie that she refrains from self harming when suicidal, as this maybe her only way of preventing suicide.

Session Outlines

_____

It will be mutually agreed that sessions will last for 50 to 60 minutes, once per week and include relevant feedback and appraisal of Katie's progress. In the interests of Katie's safety - dangerous or sharp implements, such as scissors or knives, will be removed from the therapy room. The sessions will take place at a complimentary health centre, away from distractions and noises that may interfere with my undivided attention towards my client e.g. road works or conversations. I will keep notes during and at the end of each session. We will need to agree on a written or verbal contract, in case of emergencies or cancellation of any sessions, which should be at least 24 hours notice by the counsellor or client. Cancellation notice will include holidays, sickness or any other important events.

Payment, either weekly or monthly, by cash, cheque or credit card will need to be agreed in the contract. If I decided a counselling session could not be kept, then alternative dates and times will be offered. I will also outline the absolute need for confidentiality, regarding anything revealed over the telephone or in sessions by the client.

Katie will need to agree to the release of any confidential information to my supervisor or other professionals and the criminal justice system, i.e. only where the law demands disclosure of threats to persons or property. I will establish safe boundaries and the need to exclude personal, leisure relationships, friendships, business affairs etc, from out of session contacts, as far as Katie remains my client. Anything that jeopardises the impartial therapeutic relationship may lead to complete transference and the revelation of all the client's secrets. This may leave the client more vulnerable and trust will be affected.

Suggested techniques, approaches and Models.

The CBT techniques I will employ for Katie, to treat her depression and panic disorder, are for Katie to keep a daily diary. Katie will be asked to record her day to day thoughts, feelings and behaviour in response to cues, triggers, events and the intensity of her panic attacks, self harming, suicidal ideation and depressions. A simple scale of say 1 to 10 could be used to rate the intensity of mood. Ten would be the highest intensity and Zero the lowest. Katie may learn what triggers her ill health from the intensity of the recorded mood.

I will use the Downward Arrow Technique (DAT) encompassing questions, such as, "If that were true what would that mean to you?" The DAT questioning would be in response to any core belief, assumption or thought processing that is irrational and needs challenging. If the DAT questions are met with obstruction, prevarication etc, then I would change the technique or subject of discussion.

I would set homework tasks, such as experimental behaviours, new skills, diaries etc., which would be feasible and achievable by the client. Verbal interventions would be frequent but paced using the DAT and the use of metaphoric images I would explore the meanings attributed to her own description of the metaphor, if Katie responded by describing her depression as a "black pit", "a tunnel without any light at the end" or "a cave without an exit.". Furthermore, we could imagine projecting the metaphoric images onto a large screen and she could imagine and describe the colours; shapes; noises; speech etc, in the metaphoric movie. This may help when the conversation is diminishing, the client is facing difficulty with putting ideas into words and the feelings behind the metaphoric images are intense.

We would explore the basic CBT relationships between events, how Katie thinks, how she feels emotionally and how she acts. How each part triggers the next and causes a vicious cycle which needs to be broken some point in the cycle to reduce her positive symptoms. Katie may have to change her thinking, assumptions, beliefs and actions that are fuelling her illness. One example may be that Katie holds the core belief that if she disobeys her father she would deserve to be punished. The assumption here is that she has a reasonable, caring father, which she may lack in practice.

The underpinning assumption, behind the belief about Katie's father, needs to be challenged, possibly using the DAT method.

I will introduce coping strategies to substitute her withdrawal and avoidance behaviour, when exposed to stress e.g. Katie has frequent panic attacks in busy out of town supermarkets and rushes out of the store in distress, without her shopping. I would endeavour to help Katie by suggesting for homework that she shops at a local convenience store, then at a quiet town supermarket in the evening. I will, induce the stressor by asking her to shop again at an out of town large supermarket, once the coping strategies have been achieved and Katie has gained confidence,This should be done until her behaviour improves and the fears have gone.

I may introduce a full relaxation exercise in the sessions, to be repeated over several weeks and as homework till the panic attacks have subsided in private and public places. I will suggest to Katie that she practices the relaxation exercise each time before she shops to prevent relapse. I would elicit full relaxation, calmly and clearly, in Katie by starting with her feet and gradually working up towards her face. At each stage I would request that my client tenses a body muscle and then releases the tension. Perhaps combining this with deep breathing; in and out. Imagery and alternative behaviours may be more easily and comfortably accomplished, after a full relaxation body exercise.

Using guided imagery, after relaxation, where Katie would imagine calmly walking around the aisles of the shop, selecting the products and waiting patiently at the checkout. Athletes are known to rehearse the whole activity in their minds before the event and this could work for my client.

It may help create a more positive image of a coping, confident and relaxed self in places where Katie often feels stress and panic. This would enable Katie to help change her coping mechanisms and complete her chores without panic attacks. This could also be role played within the context of the sessions, where Katie would imagine herself being relaxed and assertive when feeling angry towards her father.

The channelled anger into assertiveness may reduce the internalization of anger and help Katie, in her goal, to respect herself and act as a competent adult and not to be treated like a child.

I may introduce new coping strategies for Katie to assist with refraining from her self harming. I may recommend sucking lemons, using red markers on areas where she cuts. Also, ice cubes may be vigorously rubbed into her arms and legs; newspapers torn and ripped; cardboard boxes demolished; cushions beaten up; a mattress thrashed with her limbs - when in a lying position etc.

All of the above mentioned techniques may sway the desire to self harm, as it provides for some discomfort and aggression that is endemic to self harming. The self harm coping mechanisms are replacement therapy for self punishment. The source of her self harm is the "love betrayal", where she blamed herself for the abuse and neglect, as a child, and felt unnecessarily guilty because of her parents' neglect. The anger and hate that Katie feels towards her father is diverted from self harm and suicidal ideation, using the above methods. The alternate coping acts are a safe release of pent up emotions, substitutes self harm and may prevent a suicide attempt.

Anger, not released directly to the source, e.g.Katie's father, and internalized as repressed rage in the unconscious, is a major cause of depression and self harm, in some young people.

I will also ask Katie to write uncensored, unsent, letters concerning her experiences of abuse and neglect at the hands of her father. It would help Katie to write with her left hand, if right handed, and vise-versa, a full description of her depression and what it feels like: mental and physical symptoms. The rather illegible writing is similar in appearance to a young child's writing and allows for repressed emotions to be released.

Writing in great detail, in the form of a letter from her Child ego state with the use of her left-hand (if right-handed) to her parents will help diffuse the anger and hurt she felt when being left alone, neglected and abused.The rage and fear that causes Katie to self harm, panic, feel suicidal and feel depressed, may be safely discharged in the childlike writing. The healing of Katie happens with the cathartic release of her repressed unconscious, intense, anger and fear. that may be expressed by crying, raging or trembling etc.

We will also need to consider together the negative consequences of losing her temper with her parents and being reacted to as a "naughty" child, when grown up. Talking to her father in a relaxed and assertive, non-aggressive way, will help create better communication with her father and help her father to see Katie as an autonomous, independent young lady.

I will request that Katie attempts small tasks, when depressed and gradually build the tasks up to actions more complex. This will enable Katie to overcome the depressive inertia and help break up her sense of worthlessness, helplessness and inadequacy which are symptoms of depression. It also assists in breaking the cycle of attempting to do something big and failing, Katie may start with small tasks and gradually build on them, e.g. some small tasks can firstly be practiced at home, such as washing clothes and dusting, or in public places such as a short 10 minute walk around a town park. Any exercise will help mental health and help increase Katie's self esteem. It may also induce the release of serotonin, the natural "feel good" hormone in the brain.

Some Approaches

I may need to use certain CBT approaches and methods with my client. These may involve active listening, empathy, unconditional positive regard, good conversational skills, good eye contact, non-verbal communication and facial gestures. My basic approach will be to create a collaborative, co-operative working relationship with great trust between my client and myself. I will aim to apply this approach from the first session onwards.

I will ensure that Katie feels free to speak openly and unhindered, reinforced by my verbal and nonverbal acknowledgements and praise e.g. empathising verbally with what she says, e.g."Yes, I understand your rape ordeal must have been very distressing and traumatic for you…" This will be in response to my client's admission of being raped and her distress signals e.g. frequent crying in sessions or finding it difficult to trust me.

I would, in addition, utilise body communication: nodding and shaking head. However, I would show no visible signs of revulsion or horror, as that may convey that she is causing me to feel stressed and Katie may limit or avoid certain subjects because she may not want to "hurt" me.

I will keep my body posture open but relaxed and my voice will be in soft tones. I may summarise, paraphrase or repeat verbatim what words she has spoken. Thus I will convey empathy, understanding and genuine interest. Indeed, one must put oneself in the mindset of the client to enable accurate understanding and correct interpretation. Most importantly I will observe what is not said, rather than what Katie says. This approach is useful when the client finds it too difficult to talk freely with me in sessions. There may be painful memories, emotional scars, thoughts, emotions or past actions that inhibit the client's verbal communication. The DAT method may prove useful in such situations.

I will aim to be honest and consistent at all times, whether it is keeping to a regular schedule or being transparent, when asked about my own feelings. I will be patient in waiting for appropriate responses and being open about what each stage of treatment would involve.

I will convey presence and interest by avoiding poor eye contact or behavioural mannerisms, that may be distracting or annoying to the client. Such mannerisms may include watching the clock or my watch, folding my arms or legs in defensiveness or frowning in disagreement about what Katie conveys. I would ensure the seating of the client is at the same height as my chair, to avoid approachability or convey superiority on my part as the counsellor.

I would avoid going into agreement with Katie's father's actions or speech or any other protagonist that Katie submits, except in emergencies such as if Katie's life is in danger e.g. by suicide or domestic violence I may at this point call for an ambulance, contact her GP or Psychiatrist.

In the clinical practise, my interventions they should only be suggestive, prompting or encouraging. My perception, as a counsellor, of Katie's traumas and experiences may not always be accurate and projecting a model of the "right" conduct, as if she must act in a certain moral way, may be unethical, as this puts pressure on my client to perform in a way that they find objectionable or even offensive e.g. she should have told her teacher or the police of her rape ordeal at an earlier age. Katie is more likely to have feared physical attacks at the hands of her father, especially if she has been threatened as an abused child not to tell anyone of her abuse or face injury or even death.

Katie has had no real love or affection in her life and her trust of adults has been betrayed, it follows that she will need from the counsellor: consistent praise, positive feedback and confirmations that she is really "OK!" Katie will be able to reframe the past traumas, as not her fault and nothing to feel guilty about. The goal will be to bring about change, through reframing and putting her traumas into a new context, this allows Katie to become the confident and high self esteem adult she seeks to be in therapy.

Models of Sessions

Session 1
----

1. I will discuss the collaborative relationship between Katie and myself; working together towards a mutually agreed outcome.

2. Discuss with Katie her difficulties and offer any information, including leaflets, self help books and details of websites, e.g. Mind

3. Request Katie keeps an episodic diary of any panic attacks, phobias, depression etc, including the form they take, the duration, symptoms and responses to trigger events.

4. Review and discuss collaboratively the above.

Session 2
----

1. Review the episodic diary and discuss the causes of depression and panic attacks, such as events; thoughts; feelings and behavioral responses.

2. Focus on past thoughts, beliefs and behavioral responses that caused her to feel panic attacks or depression. Offer an alternative interpretation of distressing events in her youth and how it affected her emotional state. Offer alternative means of coping and behaving that may change the way in which she feels in her emotional state, such as discussing who or what was really responsible for her present emotional state e.g. her abusive Dad.

3. Negotiate experimental thought, feeling , beliefs
and behavioral challenging new interpretations of her present emotional state.

Sessions 3 to 7
----

1. Repeat Session 2

2, Develop new cognitive and behavioral practical coping strategies based on session 2, e.g. non - avoidant behavior in public and cognitively replacing old patterns of thinking, such as "I am guilty for the abuse I suffered." Katie may directly challenging learnt thoughts, e.g. "Any guilt or fear I experience belongs to Dad."

3. Use images(metaphors, projected onto an imagined blank screen), reframing(seeing the past traumas in a new context), refocusing(how the new contexts affect and applied to the present), and rational responses, e.g. thinking and behaving logically in the present towards stressful situations.

4. Set Katie homework based on the above, e.g. applying the logical and rational to triggers, such as challenging negative mental input of her parents directly: prompting Katie to use self talk in the positive, "Any phobia or distress belongs to you Dad and you alone."

Sessions 8 to 10
----

1. Challenging remaining negative beliefs, thinking and behavior depending on how Katie has progressed with applying the new cognitive homework in her personal and public life, e.g. "My Dad was abusive to me but I am responsible for self harming", replaced with, "My Dad was abusive to me and the self harming belongs to you Dad.Therefore, I am not guilty and am free from self hate and rage towards myself."

2. Work on avoidance, such as running out of supermarkets due to a fear stressor of crowds of people. Katie maybe fearful that others may see her self inflicted wounds. Katie could replace her social phobia with new coping strategies, based on the counsellor's empathy and absolute positive regard towards the misery and suffering that Katie feels. The counsellor may suggest several interpretations of the trigger event that may help Katie to feel less anxious, e.g. the shoppers are too busy to notice Katie; the self inflicted wounds are covered by her clothes; the wounds, if seen, may invite compassion and concern from the customers.

3. Test new cognitive and behavioral strategies by gradual exposure of stressors to Katie. Start small with One Stops, then build up step by step to larger supermarkets. Suggest Katie could be accompanied by a close friend at first and shop at quieter hours e.g. early morning or late evenings. The object is to reduce the panic attacks gradually until Katie feels confident to shop alone. Silent, positive self talk to her internalised father's negative commands may reduce the client's stress and this could be coupled with thinking of up to 6 alternative explanations,as to why Katie feels the way she does.This may develop more rational responses to her phobia in public.

4. Review episodic diary with Katie and acknowledge goals and progress made in therapy, both in and out of sessions. It is important that the client feels she is making progress and has achieved positive outcomes, otherwise Katie may give up too early before reaching her own goals..

Expected Outcomes

Greater self-awareness of Katie's mental health and successfully managed by herself.
Successful reduction of depression and panic attacks, when Katie is exposed to triggers: stressful situations, e.g. shopping alone, conversing with her parents, memories of childhood abuse etc.

Reinterpretation or reframing of past traumatic events and present stressors, e.g. her neglect as a child and current relationships with her parents. The goal is more assertiveness, less withdrawal or losing her temper with her parents.

Focusing on that which has been nurturing and a positive influence on her past and present beliefs, emotions and behavior, e.g. a school teacher giving her support with homework.

A more rational and highly developed reasoning pattern of thinking, resulting in healthier feelings and more appropriate behavior in her social and family life, Katie can apply the new cognitive pattern of thinking to any feared situations or trigger events with confidence and greater rationality.

Thus, having a real reduction in psychological relapse into depression or severe panic attacks, resulting in fewer admissions to mental health units.

Conclusion

———————

Katie can expect, as an outcome, less challenging negative thinking, feelings and behavior, and a new healthy emotional state based on "a life worth living". A life without over dependency on medication and the NHS Community Mental Health team of psychiatrists, community nurses and social workers.

Katie, without the mental baggage of the past, could realise her own goals of continuing her education, a useful occupation and psychological resolution with her past hurts and present relationships with her parents. So, a life for Katie without disabling panic attacks, depression and self harming. Thus meeting the stated goals set out in the first session of her counselling with her therapist.

ISBN-10:1539457192
ISBN-13:1978-1539457190

DEDICATION

In memory of my faithful friend Pumpkin and Carolyn for all the love we shared,
&
Rod Brans, for standing by me in the most difficult of times.

ACKNOWLEDGEMENTS

Thank you to Your Book Promoter for all your help and support.